DEMOCRATIC CENTRALISM IN ROMANIA:
A STUDY OF LOCAL COMMUNIST POLITICS

DANIEL N. NELSON

EAST EUROPEAN MONOGRAPHS, BOULDER
DISTRIBUTED BY COLUMBIA UNIVERSITY PRESS
NEW YORK

1980

320.9498
N425d

EAST EUROPEAN MONOGRAPHS, NO. LXIX

BRADFORD COLLEGE

JAN 25 1982

EAC   /4.25

— LIBRARY —

Daniel N. Nelson is Assistant Professor of
Political Science at the University of Kentucky

Copyright © 1980 by Daniel N. Nelson
Library of Congress Card Catalog Number 80-66055
ISBN 0-914710-63-X

Printed in the United States of America

CONTENTS

TABLE OF ILLUSTRATIONS	v
INTRODUCTION	ix

CHAPTER

I.	DEVELOPMENT AND DIALECTICS: AN APPROACH	1
II.	DEVELOPMENT/MODERNIZATION IN ROMANIA	11
III.	THE FRAMEWORK OF LOCAL POLITICS	26
IV.	PEOPLE'S COUNCILS	51
V.	LOCAL POLITICAL ELITES	108

CONCLUSION	145
APPENDICES	150

A.	MAP OF RESEARCH AREAS	151
B.	DEPUTY QUESTIONNAIRE	152
C.	THE DATA BASE	155

FOOTNOTES	165
BIBLIOGRAPHY	176

TABLE OF ILLUSTRATIONS

TABLE   PAGE

I.	Demographic/Social Indicators	14
II.	Economic Indicators	15
IIIa.	Population Data for Four Counties	18
IIIb.	Population Density	18
IV.	Indices of Comparative Development/ Modernization Levels	19
V.	Scaled Ranking of Counties by Indicators of Modernization/Development	20
VI.	Average Annual Rates of Change for Six Indices of Modernization/Development by County	23
VII.	Scaled Ranking of Counties According to Average Annual Rates of Change for Six Indices of Modernization/Development	24
VIII.	Romanian Territorial-Administrative Units	32
IX.	Iaşi County Leadership: Party-State Overlap	44
X.	Question Nine: Deputies' First Active Interest in Public Life	56
XI.	Question Ten: Party Membership Dates	63
XII.	Question Eleven: Deputies' Prior Public Political Activities	67
XIII.	Question Seventeen: Deputies' Opinions of Most Important Problem for People's Council	76
XIV.	Question Eighteen: Changes Needed in People's Councils According to Deputies	80
XV.	Question Nineteen: Most Important People's Council Activities for the Public in Deputies' Opinions	83
XVI.	Question Twenty: Presence of Non-Political Organizations which Influence Public Life in Opinion of Deputies	86
XVII.	Question Twenty-one: Means of Interesting Citizens in Public Life	89
XVIII.	Question Twenty-four: New Attributes of People's Councils in Opinion of Deputies	99

XIX.	Question Twenty-six: Nature of Problems	
	Raised by Citizens	104
XX.	Distribution of Elite Interviews by	
	County and Level	110
XXI.	Principal Local Problem as Indicated by	
	Sub-National Political Elites	127
XXII.	Local Political Elites' Responses to Question:	
	"Are You A Politician?"	139

DIAGRAMS

I.	Romanian Government:	
	An Organizational Representation	35
II.	Question Fourteen: Deputies' Current Non-Party	
	Organizational Activities	70

Research for this study was supported by a grant from the International Research and Exchanges Board which has, of course, no responsibility for my interpretations nor presentation of ideas.

Professors Jerome Gilison (John Hopkins), Jan F. Triska (Stanford) and Stephen Fischer-Galati (Colorado) have read the manuscript and offered valuable suggestions. I am particularly indebted to Jerome Gilison from whom I received invaluable encouragement coupled with justified criticisms while a student at The John Hopkins University.

Research assistance and typing were provided by Ms. Laura Kass and Mrs. Pat McSparren, respectively. Their efforts in my behalf are greatly appreciated.

I have dedicated this book to my wife, Joan. One of the burdens to be borne by comparativists in any field is living from suitcases in various corners of the world. Joan has made the travels of this comparativist seem easy as she accompanied me on research trips, accomplished work of her own, and provided the warmth and understanding few people can live without.

INTRODUCTION

"Development" and "modernization," in the contemporary literature of comparative politics, intuitively denote a vast array of socio-economic and political change. This study concerns the broadly-based changes to which those terms refer, but with specific emphases that need to be clarified. My attempt is to consider the relationships between socio-economic and political transformations in a communist party state by adopting a comparative sub-national focus,[1] i.e., where political institutions and society come into the closest and most continuous contact.

As a study of politics in a communist party state, this work constitutes an effort to apply fairly common assumptions about "developing/"modernizing" polities in the *non*-communist world to the case of an Eastern European state. My work is intended, therefore, to be a test of hypotheses concerning "Western" and "Third World" against the experience of a developing communist nation.

"Local" or "sub-national" politics, often in the shadows next to national or international phenomena, is my focus here, in part *precisely* because the glamour of inquiry at such levels is not so prominent; access to information, I found, was promoted as the researcher's distance from *overtly* sensitive national issues was increased.

Two other reasons for an intra-national focus, however, are important. First, despite the decline of the totalitarian model for communist politics, and the realization that more is going on than "meets the eye," most writing about such states remains nationally or internationally focused, with little credence given to the importance of local political life on the larger domestic scene or foreign policies. I contend (and believe that this work demonstrates) that intra-national comparisons of local politics allow a fuller portrayal and understanding of communist polities than that provided from the perspective of a state's capital, a national elite, central bureaucracy, etc. Furthermore, if one intends to speculate (hypothesize) about the relationships between socio-economic and political

change as have so many scholars of comparative politics, then an effort should be made to obtain comparable data from the level where political institutions and society interact the most—the local level.

Most specialized terminology used in the following work is self-explanatory. In general, I use English terms in place of Romanian ones, often including the Romanian in parentheses after the English equivalent. Where no accurate English equivalent is available, the Romanian term is used followed by an English phrase describing it, again within parentheses.

Since denotational problems with "development" and "modernization" have plagued political scientists, these terms must be clarified as well. As a manifestation of the intuitive nature of these concepts, they have been used in the literature interchangeably—a problem compounded by words such as "industrialization," "urbanization," etc.

I think of "development" and "modernization" as two distinct processes that occur together, rather than one process known by two names. Such a position is important here because the hypotheses of comparative politics regarding development and/or modernization (the applicability of which are considered by this study) suggest that these processes of change are usually simultaneous, but essentially antithetical.

Allowing for the entirely relative nature of both terms (relative in all cases to both preceding conditions and to other developing/modernizing states), about all one can say is that any change in a society's "way of life" towards greater specialization, complexity (or differentiation), secularity, and participation from any initial condition involves a society in "modernizing" change as we know it today. If modernizing means changing the manner in which a society goes about living, "developing" in broad socio-economic terms means changing what a society does, in the direction of expanding social and resource exploitation. I am, then, trying to distinguish changes in what a society accomplishes ("development" if it accomplishes more quantitatively and if its accomplishments are measurably better in terms of quality), from *how* it accomplishes tasks ("modernization" if changing towards the characteristics listed above).

While these may be analytically separable processes, neither could long endure in isolation from one another. For example, "developing" socio-

Introduction xi

economic potential seems to require, eventually, technological, organizational, and attitudinal changes characteristic of "modernization"; i.e., there is a limit to what a society with little mechanization, tribal or clan organization and spiritual orientation can do to develop social and natural resources. Similarly, it is hard to imagine a long-term success for an underdeveloped society (where its social and natural resources remain unmobilized and untapped) in any effort to change its way of life along the lines suggested above, by superficially adding technical, organizational, and attitudinal trappings. Simply put, a society cannot long have either development or modernization without the other.

The foregoing says nothing, of course, about the pace or nature of changes called "modernization" or "development" on a broad socioeconomic scale. Indeed, modernization is, by definition, a destablizing process and, once begun, can involve rapid and radical change or systemic transformation just as likely as it might be an evolutionary or gradual process. Development is often seen in a different light. Although exploiting societal and natural resources might require changing the "way of life" of a society (i.e., modernization) or bring such change even if a potentially radical modernization is *not* desired, "development" per se is regularly undertaken in the guise of conservative or reformist change. But, much to the chagrin of non-modern or anti-modernization proponents of development, mobilizing the populace to exploit resources usually brings a change in a society's way of life that increase inputs into the political system, thereby making it harder for the political system to meet demands unless it, too, "modernizes."

The political varieties of those ideas (development/modernization) are frequently used without any distinction. For some states, the ability to solve problems or meet demands, to innovate and manage change[2]—that is, its *political development*—is contingent on *political modernization*, indications of which include mass political parties, extensive bureaucracies, specialized executives, mass media, etc. For other cases, however, political development would be adversely affected by political modernization—since such accouterments are not needed for all political systems to function in a developed manner (to meet demands regularly). Yet, if socio-economic

xii   DEMOCRATIC CENTRALISM IN ROMANIA

modernization can be the "thrust" for increased demands on the political
system, it is probably correct as well to argue that a non-modernizing
polity will be, in effect, "overloaded" resulting in "decay." I think it is
better, therefore, to posit that a political system does not have to be
"modern" to be "developed"; or vice versa. Nor, for that matter, does
socio-economic modernization mean simultaneous modernization of
political life, although not changing together would create demands on
a relatively static political system.

This book's purpose, then, is to explore the relationship between socio-
economic and political changes in the Romanian case. In Chapter I, an
explication of a dialectical approach to the relationships between socio-
economic and political change is offered, followed by a second chapter
on development and modernization in Romania and a third chapter on
the framework of local politics in Romania, which is at once an introduction to the organization of the Romanian political system and the
ideological intent for sub-national political institutions. Ensuing Chapters
IV and V are addressed to a presentation and examination of information
obtained during research.

CHAPTER I
DEVELOPMENT AND DIALECTICS:
AN APPROACH

Precisely why societies and polities change is a problem by no means solved and, thus far, ill-considered by comparative politics. Contemporary (i.e., late-twentieth century) works in that field have, however, moved away from the nineteenth century legacy of social evolutionists,[3] and become increasingly congnizant that such transformations do not necessarily constitute ongoing "improvement," are not always gradual in their rate, and are not necessarily followed by equilibrating mechanisms as in a biological organism.

The dynamic of change in the politics and societies of human communities is considered obliquely by many scholars now writing comparatively, as though they realize endogenous factors promote or foster change on a massive scale, but are unable to attach typologies to them. A feature of most works on socio-economic and political change is the assumption of conflicting forces—without using the term "dialectic" per se. Scholars with all types of intellectual bents, favoring consensual or conflict images of society, utopian or rational,[4] offer a recognition of contradictory processes within what they intuitively label development and/or modernization. The primary differences among interpretations of modernization/ development turn on the question of whether or not conflict is but a passing crisis or one of a series of crises, *or* is ongoing, suffusing all of society and all of its politics (i.e., a dialectical dynamic).

In the broadest respect, a dialectical approach views the logical and historical process of events as being propelled by the interactions of opposing or conflicting elements or phases. A concomitant of Hegelian-Marxist dialectics, that these opposites must eventually be reconciled in some higher, more perfect union or synthesis, is not part of my use of the term "dialectic." Dialectical conflict appears, according to that approach, at all times in development/modernization, without reaching a synthesis. Furthermore, there is no corollary to a dialectical approach as understood here which necessarily suggests that the conflicts are among

1

economically-based social classes, nor that such conflicts inevitably require violent revolution. Rather (as used here), a dialectical approach looks, generally, to contrary tendencies for an explanation of change, and specifically to inherent ongoing conflicts between socio-economic factors called modernization/development and political change.

Examples found throughout the literature of comparative politics suggest vague relationships between socio-economic factors and political systems during modernizing/developing changes that are, most often, *not* dialectical but predecessors to a dialectic approach.

Samuel P. Huntington, for instance, fears that the impact of modernizing is a threat to political institutions, and thereby to political order. The antithetical connection is clear when he writes:

Social and economic change . . . extend political consciousness, multiply political demands, broaden political participation. These changes undermine traditional sources of political authority and traditional political institutions. . . . [5]

Political authority, and institutions which embody it, thus interact dialectically with released "socio-economic forces" such as "urbanization, increases in literacy and education, industrialization, (and) mass media expansion"—all of which connote modernization by most accepted usages.

Other political scientists express Huntington's concerns for dialectical processes in different terms:

The more effective a government in achieving rapid gains in the social and economic fields, the more it increases the level of services and benefits demanded of it. . . . The greater these burdens of government, the more likely they will exceed the capacity of government to fulfill them, particularly if the pace of economic development temporarily levels off or declines. [6]

For David Apter, it is clear "that the general process of modernization will be accompanied by periodic changes in types of political systems," because of an innate connection that he posits between socio-economic change and political phenomena. [7] Apter talks about the "tendencies in modernization" for certain types of societies and political systems to correspond to certain levels or stages of modernization. Whether a

Development and Dialectics
3

country's socio-political system, in Apter's words, moves from a "mobilization" to a "neomercantilist" society, or either of those systems to a reconciliation system,[8] conflicting interactions between the traditional and the "modern" are again implicit to that movement—not a dialectical relationship, as such, but a conviction that prefaces a dialectic approach.

John H. Kautsky argues that "certain political changes, notably the advent of modernizing regimes, lead to economic changes."[9] Kautsky makes an explicit connection between economic change in modernization and pressure on the political system:

> . . . if industrialization does proceed . . . it becomes a major threat to modernizers in power. As these advance industrialization, they, in that very process, create and strengthen new groupings, such as industrial workers and also white-collar workers and professional and semi-professional employees, and they integrate the remaining peasantry into the larger economy. Growing numbers among all these . . . become . . . organizable and aware of distinct interests in opposition to those of the modernizers in power.[10]

Crises of development are de facto dialectical concerns of Lucian Pye, too, as he first suggests the problems of government "in reaching down into the society to effect basic policies" of national development; when successful, the very attempts by a regime to change old patterns "can unleash widespread demands," or a "participation crisis." Because Pye sees change as evolutionary and is oriented toward a consensual image of society, demands for participation are followed by *integration* in his formulations of a developmental process or sequence. Nevertheless, Pye is writing about how political institutions can accommodate "popular politics," given rise through their performance.[11]

Cyril E. Black's "agony of modernization" seems related to dialectical conflict as well, although it offers a different conception from that proposed here since Black speaks only of the disruptive political results of socio-economic transformation. "When significant and rapid changes are introduced," writes Black, "no two elements of a society adapt themselves at the same rate, and the disorder may become so complete that widespread violence breaks out, large numbers of people emigrate, and normal government become impossible. . . . " Whether or not a violent

extreme is reached, the inherently de-stabilizing nature of modernizing change demands that institutions and functions change, too; but, as Black points out, "they [the institutions and functions] do not surrender without a struggle," and the dynamic of modernization, and its "agony," seem to be born from conflicting interactions of society and politics, an essential element to a dialectic approach.[12]

Like Black, Holt and Turner conclude their study of the "Political Basis of Economic Development" by noting that government direction of economic matters is met by "opposition from people in the local communities" and that "stringent measures introduced by the central authorities increase what might be called the 'propensity to revolt' in the society."[13] Again, recognition is given to the conflicts and competition generated as politically-induced efforts to control socio-economic change foster, in turn, pressures on the political system itself, yet without a specifically dialectical viewpoint (i.e., one that sees conflict as the ongoing dynamic force).

It is generally recognized, then, that a relationship exists between and among socio-economic and political changes. My suggestion is that this consensus in comparative politics identifies an essential tenet of a dialectic approach to those types of change—that is, the antithetical relationship between society and political institutions, and between the processes we call development and modernization.

The nature of "theoretical" work in comparative politics, however, has not brought us to the point of suggesting a cogent hypothesis. One can conjecturally assert the existence of a dialectical relationship among phenomena of socio-economic and political natures, thereby suggesting an answer to the question "how does development/modernization proceed," but it is far from sure how to test that relationship empirically. Thus, what we have in comparative politics are "pre-hypotheses." Joseph LaPalombara has commented on this situation by warning that

. . . we must not be deluded into thinking we have evolved empirical general theories when what we have are a number of impressionistic, somewhat abstract, deceptively empirical observations strung together by logical statements of varying elegance.[14]

Development and Dialectics   5

LaPalombara's remarks notwithstanding, Nie, Powell and Prewitt posited that a "general hypothesis" has been confirmed in early comparative studies, such as Almond and Verba's *The Civic Culture*, suggesting that "economic development alters the class and organizational structures of societies which in turn increases the level of mass political participation."[15] Conversely, others have hypothesized that a "political elite committed to economic growth may stimulate the formation of demands in the process of inducing social change."[16]

Most of the above-mentioned comments regarding the conflicting relationships between socio-economic and political changes have been based upon non-communist experiences. In studies of communist politics, however, the 1960s and 1970s have witnessed a growing awareness of what developmental or modernizing changes portend for communist-party states. Nascent hypothesizing has been a concomitant of a new-found awarness that totalitarianism cannot be the conceptual *sine qua non* of communist studies; as comparative methods have replaced Kremlinology, more recent approaches have suggested dialectical relationships in processes of change.

Richard Lowenthal focuses on the duality of goals in communist party states—an ideological utopia *vis-à-vis* rapid, successful modernization/development. That duality, Lowenthal continues, engenders further change:

The dynamics of Communist regimes in developing countries thus appear to be characterized by recurring conflicts not only between the two kinds of goals pursued by those regimes, but between two types of social change arising from their policies.[17]

Lowenthal states succinctly the pre-hypotheses with which other authors attempt to deal. Peter C. Ludz's study of party elite in the GDR, for example, begins with a recitation of these concerning the East German political system and social order. He includes the notion that

. . .GDR society is now undergoing increasing differentiation as a *result* of the industrialization process. Certain political and

6   DEMOCRATIC CENTRALISM IN ROMANIA

social conflicts *generated* by these developments are becoming dominant.[18]

Ludz, believing that "conflicts are invariably social as well as political,"[19] summarizes ten postulates in a "unifying hypothesis":

Under conditions of political, social and intellectual change, the originally totalitarian SED has tended to develop into an authoritarian party.[20]

Ludz, then, is pointing to the dialectic of development/modernization wherein socio-economic development induced by political elites (i.e., the Party in communist states) engenders socio-economic modernization that, in turn, affects the political system itself.

Dennis Pirages' considerations of "Socio-economic Development and Political Access in the Communist Party States"[21] concern the relation between *levels* of development or modernization and the political system. Investigating the hypothesis that a positive correlation exists between a society's socio-economic level and "access" to elites in the political system (that "the responsiveness of the decision-making structure should be greater and the political compliance structure should be less coercive at higher developmental levels"[22]), Pirages attempts to test an hypothesis that is not dialectical, but one which suggests a causal link between socio-economic change and political life. Because Pirages only looks at *static indices*, and fails to consider that *rates* of modernizing and developmental change may be the tie between socio-economic and political change, he is unable to find strong evidence supporting the hypothesis.

Jan Triska and Paul Johnson have considered similar issues under the broad rubric of political change within communist states. Their research, cross-national in perspective, concludes by noting that, while the "most significant variable in explaining political system stability and change in East Europe. . .Soviet security," one *endogenous* variable has an impact on political change—"economic innovation."[23]

In a similar vein, Alexander Eckstein's essay, "Economic Development and Political Change in Communist Systems" hypothesized that "the stage of economic development imposes certain imperatives of its own on any economic, political and social system, including communist

Development and Dialectics

7

ones."[24] Believing that there is "a significant degree of correlation between economic and political change," Eckstein argues to that point by identifying the dilemma which faces ideologically-based elites whose desire for "full political control" runs contrary to their quest for efficiency and rationality in socio-economic administration.[25] While a provocative essay, Eckstein's thoughts lack empirical support; one is left to speculate about the potential validity of such a position were a comparative study undertaken of the covariance between socio-economic and political change.

From many other works that concern communist politics, one can infer an approach that posits a causal relationship between political and socio-economic phenomena—among these are Ghita Ionescu's well-known *Politics of the European Communist States* and a series of which he is editor on political and social processes in Eastern Europe, H. Gordon Skilling's work on interest groups in communist party states, the many studies arising from investigations of Party leadership in a developing/ modernizing environment and role conflicts induced by such change within and around the Party, and a growing body of related work.[26]

Thus, in the literature of comparative politics there exists an ill-defined consensus that, in modernizing and/or developing changes there is (1) conflict between new and old and that (2) socio-economic and political forces are interrelated. Very few of the works cited, however, make an explicitly dialectical argument. It is the hypothesis which follows from these two points that is the focus of this study—i.e., that a developing polity "has within it the embryo of something else . . . it contains within itself its own antithesis, a 'negating' element which prevents it from remaining inert and immutable . . . it contains an objective contradiction; opposite tendencies operate within it and a mutual counteraction or 'struggle' of opposite forces or sides takes place."[27] No "synthesis" of this conflict is hypothesized, nor is a materialist basis for the protagonists in such conflict suggested.

Any hypothesis, by definition, must be testable. In the case of communist politics, success has been the exception rather than the rule in operationalizing variables, or in gaining primary source data. If empirical data are found to reflect on the dialectical approach to development, ways must be established to circumvent politically sensitive regimes. Since one is dealing with conjectural statements more akin to "pre-hypotheses" than hypotheses, however, this problem is magnified.

8   DEMOCRATIC CENTRALISM IN ROMANIA

I believe that a sub-national focus will increase the possibility of testing the dialectic hypothesis regarding developmental/modernizing changes. An *intra-national* comparison, generalizing from similarities and differences discovered among units compared, allows a degree of control for the cultural variable, and other variables that might be nation-specific in cross-cultural studies. Certainly, a goal of comparative politics is to generate cross-national studies; given the relative state of our hypothesizing, however, I think it best to "bite-off" something chewable at this point.

Local level communist politics has received attention that implies a dialectic dynamic as well. Churchward, for instance, comments that, in Soviet local government,

> gradual but fundamental social changes, such as urbanization, industrialization, the settlement of new areas, and even the enlargement of the size of agricultural units, produce adjustments in the local administrative structure. Such changes, as far as local government structure is concerned, are "objective developments," although in a larger context they might be regarded as a consequence of the remoulding of the economic environment *on the basis of conscious political decisions* (emphasis added).[28]

The important point here is that sub-national politics may provide the milieu in which evidence can be found to reflect on the common hypothesis of comparative politics discussed above. My choice was to probe the validity of the dialectic approach in the local politics of the Socialist Republic of Romania.

Romania is a communist political system in which "dezvoltare" (development) is the watchword of party policies, rationalizing considerable sacrifice, disruption, inconvenience, and/or risk. The one exception to the Party's commitment to development—the one step it is reluctant to take—is an overt concession to political change that would compromise party control of Romania's politics. Romania may be politically "developed" in the sense of regularly solving problems and meeting "inputs," but it is also a politically "anti-modernization" regime since it seeks to limit inputs from other than sanctioned sources. While the Party will accept, and has accepted the socio-economic modernization necessary for industrialization to work in the long-run, changes in the way of life in Communist

Development and Dialectics

Romania are very slow, constrained by the regime's fear that societal modernization will inevitably lead to increased demands on the political system. By slowing the pace of socio-economic modernization (relative to the pace of the country's development), the Party apparently seeks to postpone indefinitely (or at least to mitigate) the increase in political demands.

But the impetus from socio-economic development is towards what the Party wants to avoid. Societal differentiation has generated tensions that have necessitated some change; life in Romania is, today, a far cry from the Stalinist days of Gheorghe Gheorghiu-Dej. More important, for my interest, have been subtle changes and growing diversity in political life at the local level where government and people meet most directly, as the need to make room for citizen inputs (participation, if not involvement in decision-making) has grown along with the necessity to fortify the regime's legitimacy through a return to traditional administrative norms.

These subjective observations involve, of course, no test of a dialectical hypothesis. Since the essence of a dialectic is conflict between opposites, deciding about the relevance of such an approach for developmental/ modernizing change requires looking for evidence of such conflicts. Conflict leaves "traces" which can be discovered—namely, in the forms of intra-national political diversity and change. In an intra-national comparison, conducted in a structurally unitary and politically communist state, diversity and change might be expected to be minimal, if many of the measures are taken at essentially one point in time.

The validity of the dialectic approach would be supported, then,

1) if greater differentiation of opinions, concerns, knowledge, awareness, etc., of participants in local politics is detected in more rapidly developing/modernizing areas;

2) if greater differentiation of participants' and leadership backgrounds is found in more rapidly developing/modernizing areas;

3) if behavior, ideals, and social mores are observed to be more competitive in more rapidly developing/modernizing areas;

4) if more conflict between and among roles (e.g., the party ideologues vs. technical experts), organizations (e.g., party apparatus vs. state bureaucracy) or cohorts (e.g., the younger, recently assimilated

Party members vs. older, long-term Party members) is observed in more rapidly developing/modernizing areas.

The presence of such phenomena would suggest that a political result of development/modernization is conflict between a communist party and the social products of its own creation. A dialectic approach, positing from the start that a Party attempt to promote industrialization, et al. would contain within itself "the embryo of. . . its own antithesis," could then be seen as a promising route to take in further comparative studies of development/modernization.

CHAPTER II

DEVELOPMENT/MODERNIZATION IN ROMANIA

By almost every standard, Romania remains one of Europe's least socio-economically developed or modernized states. As late as the early 1970s, for example, Romania still had a per capita GNP smaller than all other states in Europe, save for Albania, Bulgaria, and Portugal, and was approximately equal to that of Yugoslavia and Cyprus—meaning, of course, that such European states as Greece, Hungary, Ireland, Poland, and Spain exceeded Romania's per capita GNP.[29]

Yet, Romania's *rate of change*, in some respects, has been greater than other of Europe's less advanced countries; it is, in fact, "developing" or "modernizing." For the purposes of this study outlined previously, the extent of that change, and intra-national differences in it, must be examined.

The Romanian regime, and its economic planners, recognize that their nation is "developing" as opposed to "developed." They utilize these terms, furthermore, in a sense that duplicates their usage in Western works of comparative politics—i.e., to connote widespread systemic changes like industrialization, urbanization, growth in literacy, mechanization of agriculture, etc. One member of the Romanian Academy of Social and Political Sciences writes, for instance, that

Romania still shows a great discrepancy when compared to the economically developed countries, as regards the level of the national income, the per capita output of some main products, her economic pattern, the level of labor productivity, of foreign trade, etc. When compared to other countries, the Romanian economy shows features typical of the developing countries. . . . In 1970 the gross national product per head of population was within the limits registered in certain developing countries which are acknowledged to belong to this category, for it amounted to about 50% of the per capita gross national product of Mexico, Argentina and Brazil

11

12   DEMOCRATIC CENTRALISM IN ROMANIA

. . . .Some 50% of the working population is employed in agriculture and the per capita yield . . .is approximately half the figure
obtained in the developed countries.[30]

Party leader Ceauşescu emphasizes the need for development and modernization at every opportunity as well. In July 1972, for instance, he noted
that achieving the social equality of a Marxist-Leninist State presupposes
the "impetuous development of the forces of production" and the Party's
complete attention to industrialization and agricultural modernization to
create a strong economic base.[31]

Covertly since the late 1950s when the first of several five-year plans
was revealed that emphasized heavy industrialization, the Romanian
regime has been engaged in an intensive effort to push, at breakneck
speed, what has now been dubbed by Party General Secretary Nicolae
Ceauşescu as "multilateral development." April, 1964 marked the Romanian Communist Party's "declaration of independence"[32] (as it has
subsequently been called) from COMECON and, thereby, Soviet plans
for Romania's future, which had called for an agricultural and natural
resource orientation for Romania's economy in a planned-for division
of labor among socialist countries. Foreign policy deviations from Warsaw
Pact norms during the 1960s and 1970s have evinced the continued
intention of Romania's leaders to pursue their autarkic economic goals
coupled with a re-emergent nationalism. Ceauşescu's pronouncements
on the subject of "development" now occupy volumes of published
works under the general title of *Romania on the Way of Constructing
a Multilaterally Developed Socialist Society.*[33]

Statistical indications of Romania's socio-economic change and level
of development/modernization are available. From a combination of
economic and social indicators, a good idea of the rapidity with which
Romania is changing can be gained. Such data, of course, do *not* suggest
that the "way of life" in Romania in socio-economic terms is modernizing as quickly as might be the case were the Party willing to allow social
transformations to proceed unhindered.

For example, if the modernization of Romanian life had no party-
imposed restraints, one could, I suggest, expect the increasing social
diversity to be mirrored in the competition of functional groups. While
nascent "interest groups" are present, their articulation of "interests"

Development/Modernization   13

(and competition among them) is certainly contrained, if not smothered. Data presented here do not, then, convey how the Party retards Romanian socio-economic modernization even while they *do* suggest the magnitude and direction of social and economic changes.

In Table I, five demographic/social indices are used which are commonly though to suggest socio-economic development and modernization.[34] An urban population increase as a percentage of the total population is an integral part of the complex process of urbanization, and indicates not only that large cities have appeared (which could occur in societies not developing or modernizing),[35] but that a large and increasing *proportion* of the whole nation lives in such cities. Declining infant mortality rates and lengthening life expectancies at birth are two statistics pointing towards the qualitative aspects of life in Romania, following from better health care of mother and child, better nutrition, etc. The percent of Romania's population enrolled in higher educational institutions reflects both an expansion of universities and/or technical institutes, and a growing need for highly skilled and professionally-trained individuals. Hospital beds per 1,000 inhabitants is one of several indices that one might choose to reflect upon the extension of advanced medical care.

The economic components of development/modernization can be delineated by several "tell-tale" indices, as is done in Table II. Almost all definitions of either development or modernization include "industrialization" as a prime component, if not the sole criterion by which such socio-economic change can be detected or measured; Daniel Lerner, Marion Levy, W.E. Moore and others posit such a relationship, with the last simply equating modernization with industrialization.[36]

Industrial employment *vis-à-vis* agricultural employment, then, is included in Table II to suggest that the working force of Romania has shifted considerably *away* from agriculture *to* other employment, in large part to industry; building, construction, and "non-productive" employment, while not included in Table II, also gained at agriculture's expense but not to the same extent. The third indicator is meant to suggest that growing industrial employment has seen a corresponding rise in the importance of factory-produced, non-agricultural goods in the Romanian economy as a whole. Gross National Product (GNP) figures must be extrapolated from other data, since the Western statistic of GNP is not used by socialist states; they do not include services as a

TABLE I

Demographic/Social Indicators

	1950	1960	1971
1. Urban Population as % of total	25.4 (est)	32.1	41.1
2. Infant Mortality (Deaths under 1 yr. per 1,000 live births)	116.7	74.6	42.4
3. Life Expectancy at Birth (Male and Female combined)	63.17 (1956)	65.96 (1961)	68.51 (1967)
4. Portion of Population enrolled in higher education (%)	0.31	0.39	0.72 (1971-72)
5. Hospital Beds per 1,000 inhabitants	4.2	7.3	8.5

Sources: *Anuarul Statistic al Republicii Socialiste România, 1972* (Bucureşti: Direcția Centrala de Statistica, 1972); *Demographic and Statistical Yearbooks of the UN* (New York: United Nations, 1950-73).

TABLE II
Economic Indicators

	1950	1960	1971
1. Industrial Employment as % of all employed	12.0	15.1	24.7
2. Agricultural Employment as % of total	74.1	65.4	46.4
3. Share of Industry in National Income (%)	44.0	44.1	60.8 (1970)
4. % of Roads Modernized (i.e., paved)	4.76 (1956)	6.68 (1959)	15.1 (1971)
5. Electrical Energy Produced (KW hrs/capita)	129.5	415.7	1,927.4
6. Motor Vehicle Production	none	12,123	74,360
7. Radio Production	none	167,000	484,000
8. Television Production	none	15,000	300,071
9. Refrigerators	none	10,548	191,619

Source: *Annuarul Statistic al Republicii România, 1972* (București: Direcția Centrala de Statistica, 1972). *Area Handbook for Romania* (Washington: Government Printing Office, 1972).

16   DEMOCRATIC CENTRALISM IN ROMANIA

"product" of labor with material goods and consider state subsidies and
taxes quite differently in computations. A 1970 publication from the
Joint Economic Committee of the U.S. Congress indicated, however, that
between 1960 and 1967, industry and handicrafts in Romania rose from
24.4 to 32.9 percent of their GNP, while agriculture and forestry declined
from 31.8 to 22.0 percent.[37]

Statistics for electrical energy, motor vehicle, radio, television, and re-
frigerator production levels are but five of many such indices that one
could choose that point to an expanding Romanian capacity and ability
to produce "advanced" items domestically—items that require trained
technicians, precision instrumentation, etc. Certainly, some qualifications
must be made; for example, the "Romanian" automobilie is but a copy
of the French Renault (models 8 and 12), and many intricate components
are still imported. Nevertheless, the Romanians produce their "Dacia" car,
jeeps, and trucks at an increasingly rapid pace, as is the case with hundreds
of other products. That the technology for an industrial expansion of that
magnitude was not initially available in Romania goes without saying.
Romania has, however, demonstrated an acumen for adapting foreign
expertise to domestic needs and resources, as is evidenced by continued
economic growth and diversification.[38]

Development/modernization have not, however, been uniform phenomena throughout Romania. There are, in the first place, variegated
levels of development and modernization, socially and economically
speaking. Second, and perhaps more important for this study, *rates* of
socio-economic change are by no means identical as seen through intra-
national comparisons.

Table IV lists ten indices of development/modernization from several
Romanian sources. None of these indices would, alone, constitute a definitive measure of development/modernization; but together there is
significant evidence to suggest the conclusions that the county Braşov,
among the four upon which this study focuses, is highly developed/mod-
ernized as Romanian sub-national units go, with Iaşi considerably less
advanced, and Cluj and Timiş rather similar in the mid-level state of
modernization and development. Statistics cited differ from those regarding Romania as a whole simply because not all data for the nation
have been, or can be divided into sub-national units. For example, whereas
the portion of the total population currently enrolled as students in higher

Development/Modernization 17

education is an illustrative statistic for nation-wide consideration, it cannot be used for comparison of counties since not all sub-national units of that size possess an institute or university.

In order that these indices be put in proper perspective, it should be noted that, among the four counties, Iași was once least populous, but now is by far the most densely populated, exceeding the other three in population according to latest records, although its area is the second smallest (see Tables IIIa and IIIb). Furthermore, the rate of increase in Iași's population is greatest among the four localities, nearing an annual average of 2.3 percent between 1966 and 1971, whereas Brașov's population increased at approximately a 1.7 percent rate—both considerably more than overall European national average. Many of the statistics in Table IV, however, are presented in terms of "per inhabitant" or "per 1,000 people," thereby controlling for differences in population among the four areas considered.

There is no simple way in which to present, cumulatively, the data of Table IV, since we do not know how to measure precisely the characteristics of developmental or modernizing socio-economic change. Lacking the capability to say how much of either quality each county possesses, one way available is portray *relative* levels of development/modernization is through an ordinal scale.[39]

Table V is such an ordinal scale, indicating socio-economc levels, using the 1-4 to suggest least to most developed/modernized among the four counties serving as foci for this study.

Suppositions are involved in constructing such a scale; for example, that a lower infant mortality and a smaller ratio of general schools to academic lyceums (high schools) are somehow indicative of higher socio-economic "levels." The indices included in both Tables IV and V, however, are not merely intuitive. Instead, these and many other potential indices suggest the capacity and performance of a system and, for my purposes here, a measure of relative "ways of life" in the Romanian counties.

An ordinal scale, however, fails to explain "the *magnitude* of the differences between elements."[40] Thus, the "means" in Table V do *not* indicate, of course, that Brașov is over two and a half times as developed/modernized as Iași. Instead, such means are a measure of central tendency among the four counties; e.g., Cluj, typically ranks between second and third (slightly more tendency towards the latter) when compared with the other three counties for the ten indices listed.

TABLE IIIa
Population Data for Four Counties
(Total Population by Census)

	1948	1956	1966	1971 (est)
Brașov	300,836	373,941	442,692	478,710
Cluj	520,073	580,344	629,746	672,384
Iași	431,586	516,635	619,027	688,369
Timiș	588,936	568,881	607,596	639,194

TABLE IIIb
Density
(Persons/km²)

	1968	1971	Ranking (1971)	Change in Density
Brașov	86.3	89.5	3	+3.2
Cluj	97.5	101.1	2	+3.6
Iași	118.8	125.9	1	+7.1
Timiș	72.0	73.7	4	+1.7

TABLE IV
Indices of Comparative Development/Modernization Levels

	Brașov	Cluj	Timiș	Iași
1. Population Urban	63.1	52.0	45.3	36.7
2. Infant Mortality (Deaths under 1 yr. per 1,000 live births)	36.1	30.3	37.3	43.1
3. % Roads Modernized (i.e., paved)	27.7	12.1	9.5	9.5
4. Road Density, Modernized km/1,000 km^2	70.3	40.3	35.9	42.0
5. % Labor Force Industrial	56.3	44.9	43.2	31.9
6. Investment Level Per Capita *and* % of National Total	4,980 lei 3.4	2,900 lei 2.8	2,880 lei 2.7	2,160 lei 2.1
7. Ratio General Schools to Academic Lyceums	12.1:1	21.3:1	14.8:1	36.6:1
8. % Pupils in Grades 9-12	19.3	18.7	17.6	9.2
9. No. Vocational (professional)	20	17	17	14
10. TV's in Use per 1,000 inhabitants	130	92	126	59

Sources: *Anuarul Statistic al Republicii Socialiste Român 1970, 1972* (București: Direcția Centrala de Statistica, 1970, 1972); *Județele Patriei* (București: Editura Academiei Republicii Socialiste România, 1972); *Județele Romaniei Socialiste* (București: Editura Politica, 1969).

TABLE V

Scaled Ranking of Counties by Indicators of Modernization/Development

	Brașov	Cluj	Timiș	Iași
1. Urban Population	4	3	2	1
2. Infant Mortality	3	4	2	1
3. % Modern Roads	4	3	3	1
4. Road Density	4	3	1.5	1.5
5. % Labor Force Industrial	4	2	1	3
6. Investment Level (combined)	4	3	2	1
7. Ratio General Schools to Academic Lyceums	4	3	2	1
8. % Pupils in Grades 9-12	4	2	3	1
9. No. Vocational (professional schools)	4	2.5	2.5	1
10. TV's in use/1,000 inhabitants	4	2	3	1
Mean Rank	3.90	2.75	2.10	1.25
Model Rank	4	3	2	1

Scale 1-4 suggests least to most "developed"/"modernized"; Source: Table IV.

Development/Modernization

In order for us to have some assurance that the modal ranks of Table V do, indeed, indicate something about the qualities of modernization and development in the four subject counties, we need to know if the ten indices give a clear picture of these processes. One may, for example, legitimately wonder whether or not the levels of urban population is in any way related to the other nine indices; it could be, one could argue, that Table V presents unassociated rankings that, cumulatively, mean nothing or (worse yet) mislead the researcher.

To measure the degree of agreement among Table V's indices as to modernization/development in Romania, the Kendall coefficient of concordance, or "W," can be used (rather than compute an exhausting series of Spearman rank-order coefficients, r_s).[41]

"W" in this case = .05.[42] We therefore can assume that, with a W = .75, the ten indices "are applying essentially the same standard" in ranking the counties under study as to their modernization/development.[43]

Having established the uneven levels of development and/or modernization in Romania, and offered an approximation of the differences among four subject counties, attention must be turned from static measures to indices of change, and rate of change. If the validity of a dialectic approach to development/modernization is to be analyzed empirically, then one is obliged to consider whether or not a type of conflict and competition, if seen to be present, follows from either the *level* at which a community exists in terms of socio-economic indicators, or the *rate* at which those indicators are changing.

In the Romanian case, this becomes an important distinction. For instance, Brașov district has long been one of the country's more industrialized-urbanized regions outside Bucharest, while Iași has been, traditionally, towards the lower end of any intuitive socio-economic scale (even Iași, however, being more "advanced" than some other areas in Romania). Were Brașov to exhibit more conflict and/or competition in its political life than Iași at the present time, the long-standing gap between their relative development/modernization would tentatively suggest the accuracy of a dialectic approach. Conversely, the dialectic approach would be viable were Iași found to be a "hotbed" of internal conflict and competition (by Romanian standards) among the four subject counties—that is, *if* Iași's *rate* of change is greatest in the four-county group. Thus, we

22   DEMOCRATIC CENTRALISM IN ROMANIA

need to consider whether conflict or competition in politics seems to be
related with socio-economic levels or with rates of modernization/devel-
opment. One must rule out one of these alternatives in order to decide,
even tentatively, about the dialectic approach.

Using many of the same categories as in Tables IV and V (not all are
available for all years), Table VI offers an indication of the relative rates
of recent (late 1960s-1970) socio-economic change among Braşov, Cluj,
Timiş, and Iaşi counties. The differences between 1971 and earlier scores
were obtained for each index, following which the mean annual rate of
change was calculated (dividing the difference by the number of years).
Each county was then scaled for six indices from 4 to 1, in Table VII,
with the county changing most positively (in the sense of socio-economic
development/modernization) being scored 4. These scores were, then,
totaled for each county, and both mean and mode were found.

As with Table V, the final means in Table VII are indicative only of
relative placement or ranking among the localities considered; e.g., Braşov's
mean of 2 suggests that it tended to place next to last among the four
in average annual rates of change for seven indices. Braşov's rate of change,
however, *most often* is the least rapid among the four localities (the modal
rank being 1).

We can be reasonably assured that the indices used are, in fact, ranking
the same thing (i.e., the rates of modernizing and development change) in
Table VII by calculating, as was done with Table V, the Kendall coefficient
of concordance, or W, and checking it for significance. In this case, W (.41)
is significant at $P = > .05 < .10$, a somewhat lower significance level than
is commonly accepted but nevertheless allowing us to infer that the
counties differ on these six variables.

While one cannot construe either Table VI or Table VII to provide an
absolute measure of socio-economic change in these four sub-national
units, there is the suggestion of an important contrast which must be
considered in the ensuing discussions; that is, while one district (Braşov)
is, and has been, markedly more developed/modernized in the qualities
used as indices, the greatest rate of change is found, at present, in Iaşi
county, the least developed/modernized among the four.

That dichotomy is important here because, if socio-economic and
political change are asserted to proceed together in dialectical fashion,

TABLE VI

Average Annual Rates of Change for Six Indices of Modernization/Development by County

Index	Brașov	Cluj	Timiș	Iași
% Pop. Urban (1968)	61.7	48.1	42.1	31.5
% Pop. Urban (1971)	63.1	52.0	45.3	36.7
% Mean Change (year)	.467	.633	1.067	1.733
% Infant Mortality (1968)	48.4	44.6	50.3	59.8
% Infant Mortality (1971)	36.1	30.3	37.3	43.1
% Mean Change (year)	4.1	4.77	4.33	5.567
% Roads Modern (1965)	22.5	14.2	8.2	8.5
% Roads Modern (1971)	27.7	12.1	9.5	9.5
% Mean Change (year)	.65	.26	.16	.125
Road Density (km) (1965)	63.6	38.3	29.1	33.6
Road Density (km) (1971)	70.3	40.3	35.9	42.0
Mean Change (km) (year)	1.12	.33	1.13	1.4
% Industrial Labor (1967)	54.2	42.3	39.7	28.0
% Industrial Labor (1971)	56.3	44.9	43.2	31.9
% Mean Change (year)	.525	.65	.875	.975
% Pupils Grade 9-12 (1968)	20.6	19.1	16.4	9.1
% Pupils Grade 9-12 (1971)	19.3	18.7	17.6	9.2
% Mean Change	−.43	−.13	.40	.03

Source: *Anuarul Statistic al Republicii Socialiste România* (București: Direcția Centrala de Statistica, 1969 and 1972).

TABLE VII

Scaled Ranking of Counties According to Average Annual Rates of Change
for Six Indices of Modernization/Development

Index	Brașov	Cluj	Timiș	Iași
Urban Population	1	3	2	4
Infant Mortality	1	3	2	4
% Roads Modernized	4	1	3	2
Road Density	2	1	3	4
% Industrial Laborers	1	2	3	4
% Pupils in Grades 9-12	1	2	4	3
Mean Rank	1.67	2.00	2.83	3.50
Modal Rank	1	2	3	4

Note: Score of 1 indicates least change, while a score of 4 indicates most change.

Development/Modernization 25

then one must consider whether political life relates dialectically to a high
absolute level of evelopment/modernization with relatively low rates of
change, to rapid change in a less developed/modernized environment, to
neither, or to both. Operating between politics and such variegated levels
of modernization/development or rates of change, a dialectic would leave
evidence of conflict or competition, which Chapters IV and V investigate.

Prior to that undertaking, Chapter III introduces the framework and
nomenclature of Romanian politics, with a focus on the Party's intentions
for local political institutions.

CHAPTER III

THE FRAMEWORK OF LOCAL POLITICS

Anyone familiar with the histories of Eastern European states or the Soviet Union would recognize that legalisms have not determined limits to governmental powers or established rules for the "workings of power." Furthermore, constitutions and laws are very much dependent for their substance on whomever authoritatively interprets such documents. Particularly when considering communist party states, that truism has led to the erroneous conclusion that further discussion of constitutions, administrative laws, etc., is fruitless.

As a matter of practice, both constitutions and administrative laws in communist party states *do* organize some political life outside the Party, identifying relevant political institutions and, in short, providing a framework. It is, of course, less a "framework" to provide channels for popular participation than to function as an instrument of penetration for the Party's efforts to mobilize the populace. Brzezinski's assessment is important in that regard:

> To a communist, a constitution is not an intricate legal arrangement organizing and limiting power and expressing certain societal norms. Rather it is a reflection of existing reality and a means of furthering the transformation of society. It is both passive and active, meaningful only within its own historical phase, and can be altered when circumstances dictate.[44]

Whether or not ones uses a term such as "instrument" or "means," it seems clear that there is (and has been) a utilitarian purpose for political "frameworks" in communist party states—namely to assure organized channels for transmitting Party decisions.

Such an intention is not "ideological," per se. Instead, it was practicality that led Marxism to be superseded by organizational principles, the obvious manifestation of which is that government has not "withered," as orthodox Marxism would have it do, but has expanded to assume greater burdens

26

Framework of Local Politics 27

imposed by political leaders. In order to maintain themselves in power, leaders in such states found that the state could not be allowed to wither, and that an institutionalization of their powers would have to be maintained and strengthened. Communist internationalism thus faded with reasserted national sovereignty, and formulas of "democratic centralism" were used to make the "dictatorship of the proletariat" rhetorically more palatable.

As communist party states have sought to develop and/or modernize, a dialectic approach contends, political change has accompanied socioeconomic change, if only incrementally so. According to such a way of thinking, conflict and competition over public policies become increasingly prevalent throughout the political system co-extensive with modernization/development, denying the Party a monopoly of political processes.

Party control over political life and assertion of its will through constitutional-legal frameworks are "lynchpins" in communist political systems; any change in the role of constitutional-legal political institutions in relation to socio-economic development/modernization would pose a serious dilemma for communist regimes. The Party leaderships of Eastern Europe are not, however, inevitably subject to the "winds" of change: they have tools with which to constrain and mold domestic political currents. In this chapter, I seek to explain the state and bureaucratic network in Romania to exemplify the functions served by constitutions, laws and administrative organization in communist states.

Romania has had, as a socialist state, three constitutions and corresponding sets of administrative laws. Each delineates periods of recent Romanian history and should be viewed in that context.

The Constitution of April, 1948, which identified Romania as a "People's Republic," was the denouement of a three-and-a-half year process (from August, 1944) during which time an infinitesimal communist party incrementally secured power. Soviet military occupation and blatant political intervention, a story told at length elsewhere,[45] gradually turned from pressure to coercion, forcing King Michael and his non-communist political allies to, first, accept disproportionate communist representation among cabinet-level leaders and, later, to submit entirely. After measures such as riots, strikes, and assassinations had brought Moscow-trianed Romanian communists into major governmental

28   DEMOCRATIC CENTRALISM IN ROMANIA

positions, Michael had little choice left, and he abdicated in December, 1947.

Between 1948 and 1952, Romania underwent a "revolution" of sorts, principally nationalization and collectivization in an atmosphere of political repression. In that five-year span, domestic politics was characterized by intracine conflict between the "Muscovite" and "nativist" factions of the Romanian Worker's Party. Ana Pauker, Vasile Luca, and Teohari Georgescu were, eventually, the losers to Gheorghe Gheorghiu-Dej's nativist faction (including Ceauşescu, Rangheţ, and others) by early 1952. Purging the Party membership in 1950 of "right-wing elements" (foreign nationals, bourgeoisie, intellectuals, etc.) aided Gheorghiu-Dej by depriving the Muscovite faction of Central Committee and local support. The conflict continued for over two more years, however, with Pauker attempting to gain peasant support by easing the collectivization drive, and Luca delivering pro-Soviet speeches in which "Romanians" were blamed for economic failure.[46] Between the end of February and May of 1952, Gheorghiu-Dej indicted Pauker, Luca, and Gheorgescu of the then-awesome crime of "deviationism," succeeded in having them removed from Party positions by the Central Committee, ans assumed the prime minister's spot in addition to his already-held office of Party First Secretary.

A short time after Gheorghiu-Dej had solidified his rule, indeed only one month after adding a "premier" to his titles, a new constitution was announced and adopted (in September, 1952) by the Grand National Assembly. As part of Gheorghiu-Dej's consolidation of power, the second constitution

consummated the conquests of the popular masses, led by the workers' class beneath the guidance of the Romanian Worker's Party, on the way to the construction of socialism . . . it consolidated the position of the workers' class and the alliance between workers and peasants. . . .[47]

This 1952 document was a close copy of the Soviet Union's 1956 constitution, and glorified the USSR with laudatory phrases. At a time when following the Soviet lead was the only healthy policy for Eastern European states, the 1952 Romanian constitution also established political sub-divisions and organs that mirrored those of their Eastern neighbor

Framework of Local Politics 29

(sixteen regions, 146 raions, 180 towns, and 4,273 communes),[48] which were to remain until 1968.

The ensuing decade, however, witnessed developments in international politics that made the 1952 Constitution more than somewhat embarrassing for the Romanian leadership, compromising as it did Romanian national pride to Soviet dominance. The withdrawal of Russian troops in 1958 and the five-year plan announced in 1960, demonstrated that the Romanians' concept of their national interest had veered sharply from accepted norms in the "Soviet bloc." Superficially, economic policy was the issue over which Romania broke with COMECON and the Warsaw Pact. A re-emergent Balkan nationalism, albeit in communist rhetoric, has generally been regarded as the more basic, while ill-defined, rationale.[49]

As early as 1961, Gheorghe Gheorghiu-Dej ordered work to begin on drafting a third constitution, under the direction of Nicolae Ceauşescu. Gheorghiu-Dej did not live to see that document promulgated, however, as he died in early 1965. A year before his death, Gheorghiu-Dej had led Romania to the so-called "declaration of independence" of April, 1964 when the Romanian Workers' Party (de facto communist party) issued a blatant rejection of economic integration plans put forth by COMECON and, implicitly, the USSR.

At the "ascension" of Ceauşescu to party leadership in 1965, a new constitution was announced, perhaps serving to demarcate the end of one era and the onset of another, but more clearly serving as part of a continuing break from the Soviet Union. Analytically, then, the 1965 constitution was functional in domestic and international politics, providing an auspicious beginning for Ceauşescu's regime, and further denoting Romania's policies as independent from the USSR and international organizations dominated by the Soviets.

These "functional" aspects to the 1965 document were evinced first, in the declaration with which it begins—i.e., that Romania is a "socialist" state—and, second, in the conspicuous omissions of any mention (laudatory or otherwise) of the Soviet Union. Article I of the Romanian Constitution makes this quite evident:

Romania is a socialist republic. The Socialist Republic of Romania is a sovereign, independent and unitary state of the working people of the towns and villages. Its territory is inalienable and indivisible.

30   DEMOCRATIC CENTRALISM IN ROMANIA

Declaring themselves to be a socialist nation was, and remains, an important psychological bargaining point for the Romanians. To be "socialist"
connotes a certain state of advancement along the ideologically-decreed
road to communism, based upon a socio-economic development and
modernization and a strong, politicized proletariat.

Allegedly, then, the 1965 Constitution was the *de jure* recognition that
Romania had been brought, by the Party, past the stage of a "people's
democracy" to "socialism." More than ever, it was asserted, Romania's
constitution mirrored the leading role of the working class in promoting
the evolution of Romanian society to an egalitarian condition wherein
all social classes and categories are merged into one sovereign and indivisible whole.[50] Ceauşescu himself asserted that the conditions for
socialism had been achieved:

> Liquidation of exploiting classes, assuring the unity of fundamental
> interests of the leading members of society, in agreement between
> individual aspirations and collective interests, have created optimum
> conditions for the cementing and blossoming of a socialist
> nation. . . .[51]

In the constitutional expression (Article II), the socialist society is
described as follows:

> The whole power in the Socialist Republic of Romania belongs
> to the people, free and masters of their destiny. People's power
> is based on the worker-peasant alliance. In close union, the
> working class—the leading class of society—the peasantry, the
> intelligentsia, and the other categories of working people, regard-
> less of nationality, build the socialist system, creating the con-
> ditions for transition to communism.

Internationally, such pronouncements carried significance since,
in 1965, only the USSR and Czechoslovakia (the latter by virtue of
its 1960 constitution) were considered to be socialist countries within
COMECON or the Warsaw Pact.[52] The emphasis on territoriality and
soverignty is likewise important, following on the heels of the Romanian Workers' Party's (renamed Communist Party at the time of the

Framework of Local Politics 31

new constitution in 1965) momentous April, 1964 statement, and perhaps prescient considering the 1968 Czech events.

The 1965 Constitution served domestic political purposes as well, as it refined the structures and stratification of authority established in earlier socialist-period constitutions. Romania is a "unitary" state, the constitution emphasizes, which is not without domestic implications. At the time when the Constitution was being written, the Hungarian minority in Romania (over 8% of its population) was allowed an "autonomous" region, and that document of 1965, while not abrogating such an arrangement, involved an implicit re-emphasis of the indivisibility of power in Romania—i.e., that "autonomy" is a concept the substance of which is determined by Bucharest. At it was, the "Magyar Autonomous Region" was eliminated three years after the new constitution was issued.

As mentioned earlier, each constitution was followed by laws concerning sub-national political organization, principally in 1949, 1957, and 1968, although many other minor changes have occurred.[53] In all cases, a Party-announced "need" for change was quickly followed by legislative enactment. For example, the law which ended the Hungarian Autonomous Region was part of a comprehensive administrative reorganization throughout Romania, announced by the Party in 1967 at its National Conference and obediently made into law by the highest legislative-representative body in Romania (the Grand National Assembly) on February 16, 1968 at an extraordinary session held two days after the Party Central Committee had met to accept the law in its final form. The 1965 Constitution and the Administrative Reorganization Law, together, thus constitute two of the three contemporary sources of sub-national political organization in Romania.

Territorial-administrative units established in the February 1968 law utilize terminology that is traditionally Romanian, setting aside "borrowed" Soviet organization. No doubt as part of a general tendency by Party leaders to emphasize "positive" Romanian history, terms such as "județ" (county or district) and "primar" (mayor) have made their way back into officially-accepted usage.

Table VIII summarizes the hierarchy of sub-national political life in that country. Over time, the number of județe (counties) will presumably

TABLE VIII
Romanian Territorial-Administrative Units

English Term	Romanian Term	No. of Units	Average Population	Average Size
COUNTY (district or department)	JUDEŢ	39	500,000 (range 200,000, 750,000)	6,100 sq.km.
BUCHAREST	BUCUREŞTI	1(a)	1,500,000	604 sq.km.
CITY (municipality or principal town)	MUNICIPIU	47(b)	80,000 est.	N/A
TOWN	ORAŞ	236	20,000 est.	N/A
COMMUNE	COMUNA	2,706	4,500	75 sq.km.
VILLAGE	SAT	13,150(c)	800–1,000	N/A

(a) of 47 cities, only Bucharest has a unique status; as one of the municipalities, Bucharest is nevertheless listed as a special case in the 1965 constitution and 1968 law, equivalent to county level government and, itself, divided into 8 sectors with 10 suburban communes.

(b) of 236 towns, 47 are declared by law to be cities by virtue of population, economic, or administrative importance.

(c) communes are composed of 2 or more villages and environs.

Framework of Local Politics 33

remain at 39, while comune (communes) can aspire, in a good socialist spirit, to be an oraş (town), and a town to be a municipality. Average populations have risen somewhat since 1968; in all cases, however, a mean population figure fails to suggest the wide range that exists. One county, Covasna, had fewer than 200,000 people in 1970, while Ilfov, Prahova, and Dolj judeţe had in excess of 700,000. Similarly, towns varied from about 5,000 people to over 50,000, cities from 30,000 to 220,000 (outside of Bucharest), and communes presented a myriad of varieties, some having the appearance and population of a town, but without the designation. The considerable range for all territorial-administrative units, therefore, should be a restraint on assumptions about any one such unit.

Romanian counties average somewhat over 2,300 square miles in area $(6,100 \text{ km}^2)$, which is more constant than are population levels. Counties are divided into communes, usually about 50, which are best equated to the American concept of "township"; a commune in Romania is not, therefore, a single population center, but instead is a territorial designation composed of two or more (sometimes as many as eleven) villages (sate). Communes are the basic unit of rural government in Romania with a "mini-capital" located in one of the villages, after which the entire commune generally derives its name.

Villages still contain over fifty percent of Romania's population. For people unfamiliar with the Balkans, it is important to remember that this part of Europe remains, in the 1970s, more "peasant" than not, more manual than mechanized, more agricultural than industrial, etc. Villages are no longer a political unit, per se, in the Romanian system (except as a component of a commune); nevertheless, their continued predominance as the principal way of life in Romania is important as a background consideration.

Most, but not all, counties of Romania have a municipality that serves as administrative capital, cultural center, transportation focus, etc. These are not necessarily uniform, since a municipality such as Braşov with nearly a quarter of a million inhabitants and diversified industry boasts a life style a far cry from another municipality and county administrative center, Focşani in Vrancea County which has fewer than 50,000 inhabitants and a primary industry of wine-making. In the more urbanized counties, two or three cities of considerable size exist, plus a half dozen

34   DEMOCRATIC CENTRALISM IN ROMANIA

towns not large enough or sufficiently industrialized to have the title "municipiu." Where no municipality is present, the county "seat" is, quite simply, the largest town.

All four counties studied here possess one municipality or more from among 47 of these "principal towns" designated by law out of 236 towns in Romania. The County of Brașov has only one city, Brașov, with 185, 259 people in 1971. Iași County also has a single municipality, the city of Iași, with a 1971 population of 187,966. The County of Cluj, by contrast, has three centers with the title "municipiu," including the city of Cluj with 205,435 in 1971, and two smaller cities (Dej and Turda). In Timiș County, one finds two municipalities, the largest being Timișoara with 195,470 people in 1971 and Lugoj being much smaller. In terms of the number of towns (orașe), however, Brașov clearly leads with nine, Timiș and Cluj each have six, and Iași county has but four. The number of towns reflects, of course, earlier-citied percentages of urban population.

Sub-national government (State and Party inclusive) in Romania is organized around the territorial-administrative divisions listed in Table VIII and detailed by the organizing and functioning law of the People's Councils of December 26, 1968, which is the third major document forming the basis for contemporary local politics in Romania. Generically, two "levels" of sub-national government exist—the county (judeţ) and local, i.e., strictly speaking, towns, cities, and communes. Only in the most general context, however, is governing a commune similar to governing a town or city. In practice, then a three-level conception of sub-national Romanian government is best, consisting of county, town and/or city, and commune; villages are not, organizationally, part of local government except insofar as they constitute part of a commune (from two to eleven in a commune).

Figure I presents a structural diagram of Romanian government. This portrayal, to be sure, is far from being comprehensive in the sense of including all State or Party organizations and it cannot, in any case, tell about the *operation* of politics. Nevertheless, as a reference device during the following chapters, Figure I will be helpful.

As one might expect in a state that calls itself "unitary" and socialist, Romanian government is structurally parallel at each stratum of the hierarchy, with sub-national units having Party and State organs on a

Framework of Local Politics   35

FIGURE I:
ROMANIAN GOVERNMENT
AN ORGANIZATIONAL REPRESENTATIONa
(Arrows Denote Formal Lines of Authority)

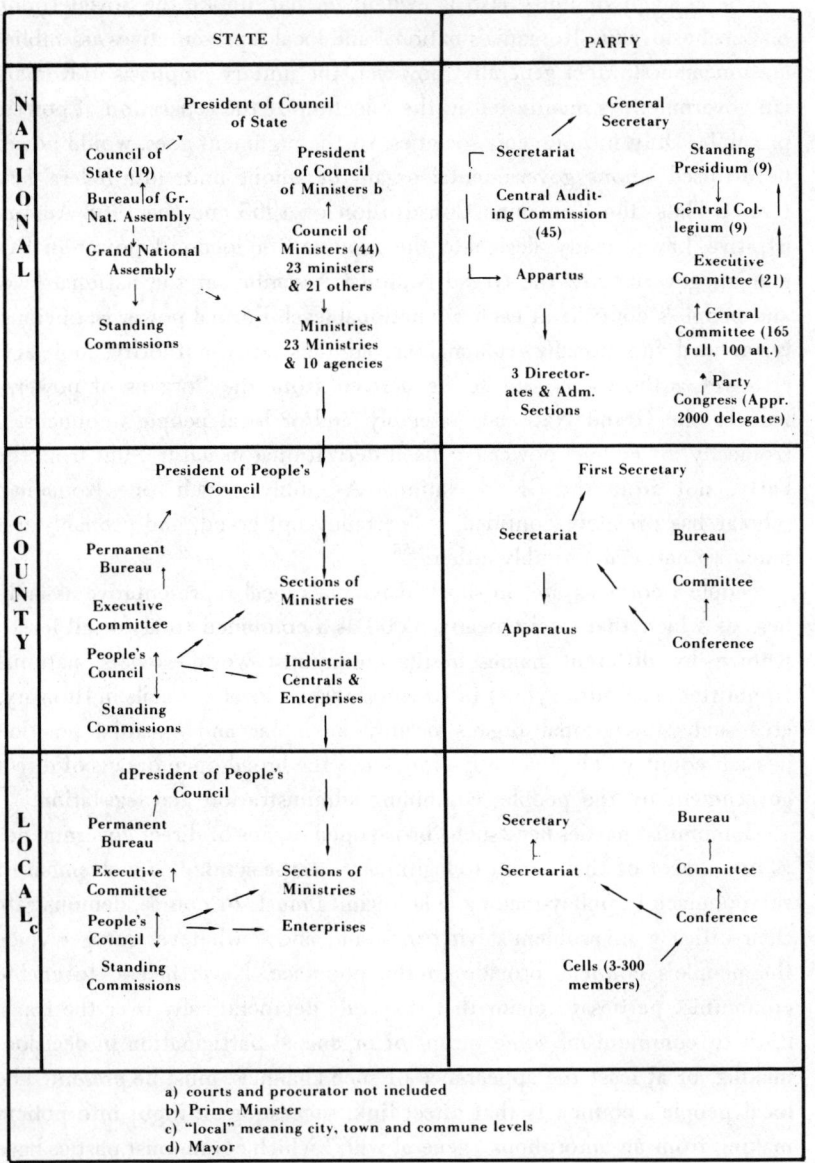

a) courts and procurator not included
b) Prime Minister
c) "local" meaning city, town and commune levels
d) Mayor

36   DEMOCRATIC CENTRALISM IN ROMANIA

miniature scale of the national bodies; only terminology changes from national to local levels—Grand National Assembly to People's Council, Council of State to Executive Committee, etc.

The concept of unity also is evident in that, unlike the Soviet Union or Czechoslovakia, Romania's national and local representatives assemblies are unicameral. Most generally, however, the unitary emphasis in Romanian government is manifested in the rejection of the separation of powers principle. Only in bourgeois societies, so the argument goes, would power be diffused among governmental organs or among units in a federal system.[54] Thus, the Romanian Constitution of 1965 and the 1968 Administrative Laws clearly designate the "source" or locus of power in Romanian government—the Grand National Assembly at the national level and people's councils at each sub-national level. Formal power is, obviously, divided functionally—rule-making, administrative authority, judiciary, etc.—yet authority is said to be derived from the "organs of power," namely the Grand National Assembly and/or local people's councils.[55] Ironically, of course, power *has* been derivational in nature, but from the Party, not from the Grand National Assembly—which, one Romanian scholar has privately confided, is "certainly not grand, and probably not much a a national assembly either."[56]

People's councils are, in short, Romania's local representative assemblies, of which there exist nearly 3,000 as a combined total for all levels. Known by different names in the communist world—soviets, national committees (narodni vybor) in Czechoslovakia, local councils in Hungary, etc.—such sub-national organs occupy a similar and essential position in each country. They are, says Ionescu, "the broad open organs of direct government by the people, combining administration and legislation."[57]

Communist parties *need* such "broad open organs of direct government" as one aspect of their claim to legitimacy—as the symbolic involvement of the populace in policy-making. The regimes must, of course, demonstrate their efficacy in problem-solving over and above whatever meager voice the people's councils provide to the populace. Nevertheless, to enable communist parties to claim that they rule democratically over the transition to communism, some means of organized participation in decision-making, or at least the appearance of such channels, must be present. The local people's council is that direct link, suggesting an input into policy-making from an amorphous "general will," which communist parties have

Framework of Local Politics 37

no more defined that did Rousseau. Yet, in writing about the people's councils in Romania, a scholar asserts:

People's Councils are the characteristic organization organs of our state. People's Councils act as part of the system of State organs of power and assure true and profound democracy, a consequence of powers of a working people's State.[58]

Under the rubric of "local organs of state power," then, people's councils are primarily charged with organizing "the participation of the citizens in the solution of state and public affairs on the local level."[59]

Representatives to people's councils, called deputies (deputați), vary greatly in number according to the population of the respective territorial-administrative unit. A judeţ can have as few as 141 deputies or as many as 231 in its people's council according to the 1968 "Organizing and Functioning Law of the People's Councils,"[60] a municipality from 81 to 211 deputies, a town from 35 to 81 and a commune from 25 to 71. Given these wide ranges, one can nevertheless estimate that a typical county would have 200 deputies, a municipality 160, a town 60, and a commune 50.[61]

These deputies meet as a people's council four times annually in sessions of several hours' duration. Between their meetings, standing commissions of the council meet in a capacity theoretically similar to committees of traditional legislative bodies. The Romanian version of these appendages to people's councils is similar to those of other Communist party states. Each standing commission (comisia permanenta) is charged with a particular "domain of activity" for which it is supposedly responsible. A standing commission is to study local problems, control branches of the national ministries or economic enterprises in their domain of activity that are locally based, and propose decisions or report on problems to the people's council or its executive committee.[62] All deputies in a people's council outside the executive committee are required to be members of one commission or another, the number of commissions and the membership per commission varying somewhat according to the level of people's council and population of the unit. A council of 200 members, for example, at a judeţ-level usually has eight standing commissions of about 22-23 members each.

38　　　　　　　　DEMOCRATIC CENTRALISM IN ROMANIA

On the other extreme, a commune-level council of fifty generally has five or six standing commissions of seven or eight members each. There is considerable similarity among county, town, city, and communal standing commissions in their titles, but some variation according to a territorial-administrative unit's economic base, level of urbanization, etc. A county people's council (or communal) will have a standing commission on agriculture and animal breeding, while municipalities, obviously, have less call for such specialties. Standing commissions on economic plan-finance, local industry-public services, construction-planning-roads, commerce, education-culture-sports, public health-labor-social insurance, and legal-administrative are common groups of domains for standing commissions in all units of government.

Each standing commission has a president, vice-president, and secretary whose backgrounds usually indicate some expertise. These individuals, like the organs over which they preside, have vaguely-defined duties, which add to the difficulty inherent to an organ which meets but for ten to twenty hours a year.

Elected from the membership of each people's council at the first session of a newly-elected council is an executive committee, and its president, first vice-president, and two or more vice-presidents. A secretary is appointed from the state bureaucracy on the basis of, increasingly, merit, but with considerable weight given to party loyalty.

Executive committees vary in absolute size, but relative to the people's council usually amount to about 10 percent of the total membership. In communes with only thirty to forty members in their people's council, the executive committee may be up to twenty-five percent of the total membership.

In the December, 1968 law, executive committees are portrayed as primarily responsible for local government on a continous basis, as a repository for powers of the council writ large; the competence of executive committees is extensive, and embody rule enforcement, social mobilization, local economic planning, maintenance of public services, etc. There are, however, no details as to *how* an executive committee will accomplish its many tasks. Particularly since executive committees meet only once a month for several hours, it becomes quickly apparent that the often-times unwieldy (two dozen members in larger cities)

Framework of Local Politics 39

executive committee is, in fact, *not* the day-to-day government. Ironically, little mention is given in the Organizing and Functioning Law of the People's Councils to the most significant state organ in terms of daily decision-making in the local community—the Permanent Bureau (Birou Permanent in Romanian, sometimes translated as Permanent Office).

Paradoxically, only a single article of the People's Councils Law of December, 1968, Number 48, is devoted to the Permanent Bureau, and even then that body's considerable prerogatives are given only oblique consideration:

The Permanent Bureau decides upon current problems, informing the executive committee on the activity carried on between meetings.[63]

Even in such an indirect statement, however, we see an indication of the permanent bureau's local power. If the permanent bureau decides on current problems and only *informs* the executive committee of its decisions, that arrangement leaves realms for potential *executive committee* action restricted to post facto considerations.

A permanent bureau is composed of the people's council president, first vice-president, other vice-presidents, and secretary. It may be a body of as many as eight individuals (i.e., with five vice-presidents) or as few as four when, as in some communes, there is no first vice-president. Regularly scheduled weekly meetings of two or more hours are the prime contact among these men as an official organ of state, but in practice they have daily contact as they work in a single government building, usually divided in half (physically and functionally) between Party and State. Yet, one should take note that such arrangements differ from most cases in other Eastern European states and the Soviet Union save for the most rural locales. Usually, care is taken in other communist systems to separate Party and state in a physical sense.

Together with the Party bureau and secretariat in each territorial-administrative unit, the permanent bureau of the people's council denotes a local political elite (to be investigated in Chapter V) that constitutes day-to-day "government" at sub-national levels. Within that political elite, and specifically in the person of the people's council president, who is always simultaneously the local party chairman (first secretary), Party

DEMOCRATIC CENTRALISM IN ROMANIA

and State merge, epitomizing the interlocking nature of communist government.

More than in any other communist party state, Romanian laws emphasize the dominant role of the Party—or perhaps *insist* is more accurate since the P.C.R. (Partidul Comunist Român) proclaims its integral presence in all government and administration not once, but repeatedly, in the Constitution of 1965. This insistence takes various forms:

In the Socialist Republic of Romania, the leading political force of the whole of society is the Romanian Communist Party (Article 3).

The most advanced and conscious citizens from the ranks of the workers, peasants, intellectuals, and other categories of working people unite in the Romanian Communist Party, the highest form of organization of the working class, its vanguard detachment. . . . The Romanian Communist Party expresses and loyally serves the aspirations and vital interests of the people, implements the role of leader in all the fields of socialist construction, and directs the activity of the mass and public organizations and of the state bodies (Article 26).[64]

Not satisfied with these provisions, the national leadership apparently decided to assure the Party's primacy at local levels through the many changes first announced in late 1967. Measures effected in 1968 institutionalized the unity of power at sub-national levels as Ceaușescu had done earlier at the national level by assuming the titular presidency of Romania (President of the Council of State) while continuing as Party General Secretary. In December of 1967, as he delivered his "Report to the National Conference of the Romanian Communist Party," Ceaușescu announced the leadership's plans to have such laws passed:

Improving the work of government on the local plan necessitates setting aside the parallelism and superimposition that are presently manifest in the activities of territorial party organs and people's councils, assuring better use of cadre. . . and resolving leadership problems smoothly and with greater competence. . . . In this regard, it is proposed that the first secretary of the county or town

Framework of Local Politics   41

party committee must be elected, simultaneously, as president of
the county or town people's council.[65]

Therefore, by fiat as much as by legislative enactment, *every* level of
Romanian government can boast that the Party and State are formally
united in the person of a local party chairman, who is obliged to be,
simultaneously, president of the people's council. At the same time,
Ceauşescu went on to insist that Party cadres must fulfill the functions
of government in local administrative organs,[66] so that the net intent
of this "proposal" was to solidify the party presence in policy-implementation machinery across the whole gamut of Romanian government.
That the Party found such measures necessary to assure that communists
not only made rules but enforced them as well, is important for this study;
changes of 1968 as cited above could be construed as one form of evidence
that, in vigorously pursuing goals of development/modernization, the
Party had given impetus to at least an enlargement of state and/or bureaucratic powers, and perhaps had re-kindled politics by providing both a
cause and an arena for conflict and competition over public policies.

Official rationales for the 1967-1968 changes were that, quite simply,
the old territorial-administrative system was not working, that the governmental organs operating within such units were inefficient, and that
duplication of party and state efforts was wasteful.[67] To be sure, party
spokesman did not always indict the old system and organs in quite such
blatant terms; criticism by means of implication was much more common
during 1967 as various journal articles alluded to the great and expanding
tasks facing sub-national government.[68]

After sufficient preparatory "discussion" about the need for change,
the Central Committee of the PCR met in early October, 1967, voted on
what was laid before it by the Standing Presidium, and the National
Conference of December 6-8, 1967 gave a final stamp of approval to
planned organizational changes (a conference instead of a "congress"
being a semantical way to avoid electing a new Central Committee). In
1968, then, the Grand National Assembly first passed an enabling constitutional amendment and subsequently voted into law both the territorial
changes (Law no. 2 of February 16, 1968) and the Organizing and Functioning Law of People's Councils (Law no. 57 of December 26, 1968).

42 DEMOCRATIC CENTRALISM IN ROMANIA

Elections of early March, 1969, consummated the transformation begun almost two years earlier.

Official rationales notwithstanding, the central tendency of all these alterations was *as much* the strengthening of party controls as promoting efficiency, uniformity, etc., in developmental/modernizing efforts. That the changes seem to embody aspects of *both* motivations is suggestive that socio-economic and political changes might be dialectically related —that the very processes of change in a society and polity find dynamics in internal conflicts.

The sub-national organization of the Romanian Communist Party is structured in a manner that parallels state organs (or vice versa), the principal exception being the Party's basic unit. In mid-1972 there were 64,500 communist party "cells," plus 6,980 party organizations in enterprises and other socio-economic units, for a total of 71,480 basic party units, leading Ceaușescu to assert that no economic or social unit exists in Romania without a party organization.[69] These thousands of units are to be found in factories, schools, offices, cooperatives, artistic ensembles, military units, residential areas, etc.—typically, wherever three or more party members live or work. Basic party units tend to be much larger, of course, up to a maximum of three hundred while most have fewer than fifty members. The essential activities of cells in Romania mirror those of basic party units in other communist states—recruitment, propaganda-education, "watchdog" operations, and organizational functions predominate.[70] Party cells have an executive leadership of sorts in the form of an elected "committee," "bureau," and "secretary" for larger cells, just the latter two for most basic party units, and only a secretary and a deputy secretary, sans bureau, for the very small cells.

Local party *conferences* are quadrennial for county and city organizations, and biennial for lower territorial-administrative units (towns and communes). These sessions are attended by, with the exception of county-level conferences, the elected delegates from the party's primary units, and constitute the local equivalent of a national party congress. The county-level party conference, on the other hand, is convened with delegates elected by city, town, and commune conferences. As at the national level, such meetings elect (or assent to) a *committee*, which, like the Central Committee of the P.C.R., is to meet four times annually to

Framework of Local Politics 43

provide executive leadership. County-level committees most often approximate 120 members.

This authority, however, is delegated to a smaller organ—.a *bureau*—of, perhaps, one-fifth to one-tenth the committee's size, which meets weekly. The Committee also elects secretaries, who together constitute the *secretariat* of five or more members, including a first secretary (or local party chairman for that territorial-administrative unit), a first vice-chairman, and at least three vice-chairmen, the latter three often called, simply, secretaries.

Membership in the secretariat and bureau and people's council permanent bureau overlap considerably, as is the case with the national level (the members of the Secretariat, Standing Presidium, and the Council of State cross-over). Although such an interlocking leadership is common to communist party states, one should remember that a local party chairman in Romania is required to be president of the local people's council; in the USSR, by constrast, the state may be "represented" in the party bureau by the soviet's executive committee chairman, but not in the secretariat. The first secretary (i.e., chairman) and other secretaries are included in a local party bureau with other "notables" such as division heads of the secretariat, the Young Communist chairman, the local party newspaper editor, the police chief, and a few others.

The complexity of these interlocking hierarchies may be illustrated by a pertinent example. In the county of Iași, in 1973, the following eight men composed the permanent bureau of the people's council, holding the offices of state indicated in column two, while filling the party roles in column three (Table IX). Note that three men are secretaries of the local PCR, two are members of the party bureau, but not the secretariat, and three are simply party members. Except at the commune level, non-party members are always excluded from election to the Permanent Bureau. Secretaries not in the state organs are members of the party bureau, and the party chairman (or first secretary) is in all three—people's council permanent bureau, party bureau and, of course, party secretariat.

This list is an example of a "formula" to which sub-national units in Romania invariably adhere: the people's council president and first party secretary are combined in one person, the first vice-president of the people's council is a local party bureau member but *not* a party secretary,

TABLE IX

Iași County Leadership: Party-State Overlap

Name	People's Council Role	Party Role
Vasile Potop	President	Chairman (or 1st Secretary) of County PCR Committee and Member of Central Committee
Gheorghe Brehuescu	First Vice-President	Member County Party Bureau
Ioan Crațu	Vice-President	Secretary County PCR
Petru Milcomete	Vice-President	Secretary County PCR
Lucian Hatmanu	Vice-President	Member County Party Bureau
Vasile Jitar	Vice-President	Member, Party
Stefan Vrinceanu	Vice-President	Member, Party
Gheorghe Zaharia	Secretary	Member, Party

Framework of Local Politics 45

two vice-presidents are party secretaries and other vice-presidents and the secretary of the people's council are lower ranking party members (although certainly not mere rank and file).

In practice, this division of roles means that, although party secretaries and the first secretary hold positions in the people's council permanent bureau, the highest state organ, they do not fill those state offices on a day-to-day basis. Instead, their offices exist (physically-speaking), and their daily work is conducted, in the P.C.R. headquarters for that territorial-administrative unit. The three individuals on whom state functions fall are the first vice-president of the people's council, usually a lesser party official (party bureau member, but not in the secretariat), a vice-president and the people's council secretary, the latter two holding no important party posts. These three men, or two men in smaller units, maintain offices in the people's council headquarters, and work there daily.

The "nature" of these party structures is clearly hierarchical and, what is more important, centralized. While the Romanian Communist Party has adopted certain traits that differ from other communist party states (e.g., the mandatory intergration of party and state indicated above), its organization remains essentially Leninist. A communist's penchant for organization, derived from early revolutionary necessity and codified by Lenin (first in *What Is To Be Done?*), is retained by the present-day party in Romania. The vertical network is distinctly hierarchical, with the nucleus of a superior organ directing the next lower stratum,[71] and an extensive horizontal network of front organizations, youth groups, etc., is maintained. Given these facets of the Romanian party, it is more important to relate the local party to the "issue" raised in this study —that is, does a dialectic approach offer a helpful way of looking at developmental/modernizing change in communist party states?

It is, in fact, the very organizational credo of communist parties which suggests an approach to politics in these states. If, as Lenin said, "being organized is unity of action,"[72] then when a communist party's "unity of action" can be seen to have been disrupted or materially altered by conditions of either high *levels* of socio-economic development or *rapid* (developing/modernizing) change, this would be tentative supporting evidence for an hypothesis focusing on the "dialectics" of development.

46 DEMOCRATIC CENTRALISM IN ROMANIA

That such disunity might be a "price" the party has paid and is paying for fostering development/modernization, is suggested by Nicolae Ceauşescu's comments:

> ...We should not ignore an unwelcome sight which is clearly evident—the fact that not all organs of collective government of the party and state have developed their activities in a similar manner ....At the same time we must watch so that this does not go the way of an increase in the number of sessions, to unending discussions, or to meaningless words. Collective work presupposes organization, discipline, firm application, and no disparaging of decisions that have been adopted...decisions are obligatory for all members of the party and no one can be permitted to disobey them.[73]

That the General Secretary found it necessary to reflect on these problems in public might indicate that the party does face difficulties of a substantial nature. Certainly, the growth of the PCR (which may also relate in some respects to development/modernization efforts) has brought large numbers of heretofore socially unacceptable (i.e., people without proletarian backgrounds) individuals into the party. Now numbering about 2,300,000 in a population of 21,000,000, the P.C.R. accounts for one of every nine Romanians, and more than one of seven adults, making it one of the largest communist parties in Europe in proportion to the population. In only ten years, the party increased from just over one million and seven percent of the population to the current levels. From one thousand members in 1944, these figures represent an almost geometric expansion.

The fourth local institution of government is the state bureaucracy, specifically local "sections" of a national ministry or economic unit, that act as junior partners to parent units in Bucharest. In the municipality or major town which serves as administrative capital of each county, and in other towns, sections of ministries have offices, staffed by professional administrators who owe their position to a judicious combination of training and party loyalty. In the parlance of both the Romanian Constitution of 1965 and the Organizing and Functioning Law of 1968, however, the state bureaucracy is known by the phrase "specialized local bodies of the state administration."

Framework of Local Politics   47

Article 51 of the Organizing and Functioning Law of the People's Councils indicates that local bodies of the state bureaucracy are to be organized in financial, agricultural, educational, health, labor, and cultural realms. In practice, the Council of Ministers decreed that particular local organs of administration will be organized at particular levels, as follows:

County: General Directorate for Agriculture, Food Industry, Forestry and Water; Commercial Directory; Health Directory; School Inspectorate; Financial Administration; Directory of Labor and Social Welfare; Committee for Culture and Art; County Office of Tourism.

City: Financial Administration; Committee for Culture and Art

Bucharest
Sectors: Committee for Culture and Art; Financial District

Town: Committee for Culture and Art; Financial Office.[74]

A euphemism such as "specialized local bodies of state administation" is considered appropriate since these bodies are created in the image of "double subordination." This formula is, quite clearly, a cousin to "democratic centralism" as both allude to the goal of local autonomy without offering any concession to decentralized policy-making, a concession that would be antithetical to the economic and social policies of communist regimes.[75] Article 52 of the December, 1968 Law spells out such a formula:

The specialized local bodies of the state administration are subordinated to the people's councils and to their executive committees. Concurrently, they are subordinated to the specialized local and central bodies.

The onus from both an ideological commitment and social pressure to democratize is thus mitigated by handing to people's councils *responsibilities* regarding "local bodies of state administration" without giving

48 DEMOCRATIC CENTRALISM IN ROMANIA

corresponding control. Repeatedly, executive committees of people's councils are charged with duties that involve "collaborating with the specialized central bodies and the local bodies of cooperation."[76] The Romanians recognize in their constitution and administrative law the centrifugal and centripetal tendencies in intra-national politics, and suggest that centralism and autonomy can be "harmonized" as a "bivalent principle" promoting social development.[77]

It is, perhaps, a moot point as to the precise meaning of "subordination" in such a legal context; if that term is used to mean "guided, directed and controlled" (which the Romanians do in Article 52 of the December, 1968 Law), the P.C.R. must be included as, at least, one of a triumverate to which the state bureaucracy is subordinate.

The "key" to party efforts to maintain control over administrative organs is the remnant of the nomenklatura,[78] whereby the party committee for any territorial-administrative unit holds final approval authority for appointment to or removal from a certain list of positions of state, social, cultural, or economic importance.

Originally, the Romanian idea of nomenklatura was a comprehensive list of "posts of responsibility" including (in 1953) "head of departments attached to the executive committees of the regional, city, and raion people's councils."[79] These positions and many others could not be filled without the consent of whatever party committee held jurisdiction.

The nomenklatura "institution" (or, at least, "regularized procedure") has decreased in importance in Eastern Europe even more rapidly than in the USSR, argues Ionescu, because as decades pass, controls and procedures "mellow" (my word, not his), and because the parties are losing their omnipotence, and are being "forced to accept collaboration with other organs and institutions."[80] If the state bureaucracy *is* gaining autonomy, one is led to ask why, and to consider the potential explanatory power of a dialectic approach. If the appointment and review of bureaucrats is no longer solely at the discretion of a local party committee, then "guiding directions" of the party might have been, or will soon be, rendered inoperative by "the very success of the regime":[81]

. . . the very effort to control the side effects of the main mobilization effort gives rise to *bureaucracies, institutions* and *loyalties*

Framework of Local Politics 49

> with dynamics of their own. . . . A group or class of people that
> the regime has created for purely instrumental purposes *develops
> independent interests* and policies designed to. . . make adjust-
> ments in its own favor.[82]

There is a good chance, therefore, to find evidence that socio-economic-
generated conflicts *internal* to political institutions are of greater import-
nace than the demands generated by such changes outside those institutions.

Interactions among all political institutions (discussed in this chapter)
in policy-making are governed by a set of constitutional-legal provisions,
a set of creeds by which decision-making in communist party states is
said to proceed, and the requirements of party supremacy. The last of
these, quite clearly, has been the predominant factor—that is, the party
has consciously molded constitution, law, and operating formulas to its
perceived needs.

The Romanian Constitution of 1965 and administrative laws assert
that authority for Romanian government is derived from people's councils,
that such councils democratically elect executive committees and permanent bureaus, that the people's councils' standing commissions study
and recommend legislation, and that the local branches of national ministries are as subordinate to the councils as to the next higher level of
the same ministry.

Furthermore, concomitant with these assertions, are creeds (which
allegedly govern the interactions of political institutions) such as democratic-centralism, double-subordination, collective decision-making and
local autonomy, which are repeatedly emphasized in party pronouncements, in the national and local press, and by national and local leaders.
This is not to say that these concepts can "peacefully coexist" anywhere
but in the minds of party leaders. "Double-subordination," for instance,
does not bode well for "centralism," democratic or not.

But the party and its perceived needs have pre-empted professions of
constitutionalism, democratic-centralism, etc., meaning that these form-
ulae have had only tangential importance for political life in Romania;
public policy has not been decided through processes of legislative debate
and enactment in representative assemblies elected in a freely competitive
contest. Instead, the day-to-day functioning of local Romanian government

50   DEMOCRATIC CENTRALISM IN ROMANIA

has been characterized by a close union of Party and State and a small group of leaders found in the Party Bureau, Party Secretariat and People's Council permanent bureau who effectively decide day-to-day issues within the context of policies established by hierarchically superior Party organs. In all of this, there is the clear implication that a conscious priority is given to the implementation of policy decisions from "above" rather than needs from "below."

If a dialectic approach is correct, then conflict and competition corresponding to either or both the rate or level of socio-economic development/modernization will bring changes to the interactions of local political institutions. These changes are not necessarily to be found in a separation of party and state, or in a diffusion of decision-making. Instead, what one can expect (if the dialectic approach is accurate) is evidence that policy-decisions are increasingly debated, that differing opinions on the priority of concerns for local government are increasingly apparent, and that observations about local political life are more diverse in those localities with either or both a higher level of development/modernization or a greater rate of change in that direction.

CHAPTER IV
PEOPLE'S COUNCILS

A: INTRODUCTION

Romania's development is not, as we have seen, intra-nationally uniform either in terms of static indices or rates of change. If the dialectical hypothesis suggested in Chapter I is correct, then political competition and/or conflict should vary with a region's *level* of development/modernization or the *rates of* (developmental/modernizing) *change*, or both. This chapter is an effort to find evidence concerning such an hypothesized relationship using data derived from a survey of people's councils deputies.

There are approximately 165,000 deputies to people's councils in Romania, if one considers all territorial-administrative levels. After the 1969 elections, 7,818 deputies were at the county level, 369 for the municipality of Bucharest, 7,358 in people's councils of other municipalities, 1,208 in sectors of Bucharest, 11,375 for smaller towns, and nearly 137,000 deputies at the communal level.[83] For this study, interviews were conducted with over 250 deputies and local political elites (the deputy sample is discussed in Appendix C).

In a population approaching 22,000,000, about 1.2% of eligible voters in Romania are deputies to one or another people's council. Deputies constitute, symbolically at least, the broad contact with the masses necessary for ideological consistency in communist party states; they allow the claim by party leadership that centralism is pursued and maintained only from a democratic "base." One should remember, however, that other states have a considerably higher level of participation in local government—i.e., France, where 1.8% of the electorate are municipal councilors.[84] Notwithstanding such a comparison, the participation of

51

52 DEMOCRATIC CENTRALISM IN ROMANIA

citizens in people's councils as deputies is necessary for not only the Romanian regime, but other communist governments as well, as long as the image of representative assemblies is useful for the Party.

Behind the facade of representative democracy, however, different mechanisms operate. Before considering the responses obtained from deputies in the course of interviews, it is necessary to point out these less-obvious influences on a deputy's position in the Romanian political system.

B: BECOMING A DEPUTY

Elections for deputies at all levels are carefully planned by the Romanian Communist Party. The links between the Party's leadership and election outcomes are not difficult to follow. The principal medium for party control of electoral politics is the Socialist Unity Front (Frontul Unitaţii Socialiste), or SUF.[85] In October, 1968, this organization was inaugurated by the PCR's national leadership (and legally confirmed in November of that year) as a revitalized coalition of all mass organizations in Romania —of which there are a great number.[86] The SUF replaced the People's Democratic Front (Frontul Popular Democratic) which had been a creation of the early communist years, originally designed to amalgamate all anti-fascist parties, and later to siphon off the political influence of labor unions, cooperatives, scientific, professional or cultural organizations, religious groups, ethnic councils, etc. Over the years, the Democratic Front had atrophied, unneeded by the PCR for anything more than appearances.

One effect of the political reorganizations of 1968, however, was to impress upon the Party leadership a renewed need for an electoral control mechanism to assure that sub-national political change would not portend a movement away from Party control. There was, moreover, an advantage for a renewed front organization from the Party's perspective. The changes of 1968 could be given more the appearance of genuinely democratic transformations if the electoral process passed through an entity that somehow subsumed Romania's many mass organizations. Again, one

People's Councils

sees an attempt by a ruling communist party to create political institutions which foster the illusion that the Party is united with a "general will" or public interest.

Thus, the SUF was created around a "national council" in Bucharest, with Nicolae Ceaușescu as its chairman, and Gheorghe Maurer (the premier) its first vice-chairman. From its inception, the SUF was an appendage of the Party, powerless, really, aside from the PCR. While sub-national SUF organizations (called councils at the county, municipal, town, and communal levels) are less integrated with the Party leadership, there is no questionff that the Front's chairman and council are responsible to the Party chairman in each locality.

The "executive bureau" of the SUF council for each territorial-administrative unit is intertwined by its membership with both the people's council permanent bureau and the Party's bureau. That being so, the requirement that every person suggested as a candidate for deputy must obtain an official nomination from the SUF organization (at the level at which he or she is a candidate) means, in practice, total Party control over who is to become a deputy. No matter what organization, group or individual suggests a person as a potential candidate, an initial process which is itself restricted by PCR control over other mass organizations, the SUF nomination is a prerequisite for being placed on the ballot. And, since the Socialist Party Front offers the only ballot, endorsed or not, there is no way of becoming a deputy without the Front's (i.e., Party's) acceptance.

Were such an electoral system the only factor to be considered when assessing deputies' position in Romanian politics, a deputy's independence might seem to be compromised but not eliminated. Once having become a deputy, however, an individual has few opportunities to express any differing ideas he might have about public policy, and the pressures against doing so are, in most cases, overwhelming.

In the first place, the people elected to be deputies are usually, but not always, party members. Hence, the onus of party discipline is enough to convince most deputies that attempts to alter what they might consider to be bad public policies is counter-productive in terms of one's career, standard of living, etc. A similar cost-benefit analysis probably suffices to

54 DEMOCRATIC CENTRALISM IN ROMANIA

reduce the independence of even those deputies who are not party members. The second inhibitor to a deputy's independence is, quite simply, the lack of opportunities to voice ideas. As a member of a state organ that meets for perhaps twelve hours annually, there is little chance to do more than listen to a few reports or cast assenting votes to decisions previously made by the permanent bureau of the council (which, for the most part, overlaps in membership with the local party bureau).

Thus, mechanisms extant today seemingly have been constructed to, first, screen out potentially restive individuals and, second, to restrict the channels available for anything more than quiescent political behavior on the part of people's council deputies.

The composition of each people's council is determined such that they are, in many respects, mirror-images of the local populations, particularly with respect to ethnic background and base occupation. (As will be noted later, however, more "sensitive" criteria such as political background and educational levels distinguish deputies from the population as a whole.) Age and sex are criteria less rigidly adhered to in molding the composition of people's councils, but also play a role. Thus, Romanian people's councils are not merely non-random in their membership—a common phenomenon in legislative bodies where "over-representation" of some social groups is present (lawyers, for instance, in the United States). In the Romanian case, like other communist party states, there is a quota-type of non-random selection for people's council membership.

Local party leaders' control of a council's membership is most far-reaching through such a quota arrangement. Electoral procedures dominated by the SUF, already discussed, screen potential deputies, and the party disciplines deputies once they are "elected." *Prior* to reaching the SUF for nomination, however, the proposal of an individual to the SUF involves: (1) a detailed consideration of his or her political acceptability, and (2) whether or not the person in question would fit into the quota. For example, between elections, a certain people's council might "need" a female intellectual over forty years of age of Hungarian descent to replace a deceased council member, in the sense that such a new member would bring proportions of those characteristics in the council's overall composition closer to the proportions held by those same characteristics in the population.

People's council deputies in Romania are, then, constrained by a quota selection system, SUF nominating monopoly, and party discipline. Taken

People's Councils   55

together, these mechanisms constitute formidable obstacles to the expression of diverse or conflicting viewpoints from deputies. One is led, therefore to be skeptical about finding evidence supporting the dialectic approach.

C: THE POLITICAL BACKGROUND OF DEPUTIES

Deputies were asked several questions which were meant to ascertain the backgrounds and experiences of people's council members beyond basic demographic characteristics (see Appendix B and C, Deputy Questionnaire and the Data Base, respectively). If a dialectical hypothesis is to be supported, then the type of people who become deputies should vary among the researched counties, and such diversity should co-vary with relative *levels* of development/modernization or *rates* of such socioeconomic changes. Particularly important here would be evidence suggesting that counties as socio-economically distinct as Brașov and Iași tend to be unalike in the kinds and extent of experiences and involvement mentioned by their deputies.

I sought an indication of deputies' first interest and/or involvement in politics by asking, "When did your interest in public life begin?" Such a question solicits information about a subject that might have otherwise (if stated more directly) engendered less-than-frank responses. Because voting and other "passive" political behavior is routinized in communist party states, the question sought a measure of the onset of "active" political behavior.[87]

If the subject did *not* immediately offer a response denoting a particular age at which first interest/involvement occurred, I would then ask an additional question to elicit a precise response. Conversely, if a deputy stated an age, I would follow with an inquiry into the circumstances surrounding that first interest. Using this response-keyed procedure, I gained structured data on the ages at which deputies first became politically interested and unstructured information on how or why that came about.

Table X summarizes the structured response given by deputies, separated into the age categories of adolescent, young adult, and mature. A fourth category, elderly (batrin), is not included in this table despite its presence on the questionnaire since no deputy gave that response. The

TABLE X

Question Nine: Deputies' First Active Interest in Public Life

Category of Answer	N = 37 Timiş % (weighted)	N = 47 Cluj % (weighted)	N = 50 Braşov % (weighted)	N = 64 Iaşi % (weighted)
Adolescent (under 20)	11.8	5.2	31.3	9.8
Young Adult (20-30)	71.5	79.6	55.1	57.2
Mature (over 30)	16.7	15.1	13.6	33.0
Totals	100.0%	99.9%	100.0%	100.0%

n = 198
(P ≤ .001)

People's Councils 57

preponderant central tendency (in both the raw and weighted data) is that present-day deputies began active political involvement as young adults. Relatively few, then, had noteworthy political experience in their high school (lyceum) years or, evidently, until they had begun working or had entered a university.

Notwithstanding such a central tendency, differences among counties are apparent, particularly insofar as Braşov and Iaşi deputies seem to exhibit contrasting tendencies—Braşov shows a markedly higher weighted percentage in the adolescent category, while Iaşi is much higher in the "mature" classification. Meanwhile, both Timiş and Cluj evidence a greater central tendency towards the 20-30-year-old category.

One can infer that political interest and involvement generally begin earlier in Braşov county for individuals who later become deputies than in Iaşi where the tendency is to recall a later beginning to political interests. In Timiş and, particularly, Cluj counties, there is greater uniformity as to the onset of political interests and involvement, with a considerably larger percentage of the weighted sample in those two counties regarding their young adult years (20-30) as the period of first political interest than in either Braşov or Iaşi.

Any expectations one might have had about uniform political backgrounds and experiences among deputies in a communist-party state are, therefore, contradicted by these data which, at least, *suggest* the inverse. Furthermore, the pattern of diversity among responses seems to vary directly with a similar pattern implied in Chapter II—where Braşov was found to be the county most developed/modernized, while Iaşi was changing more quickly, and Cluj and Timiş counties were mid-range in both respects.

Seeking an explanation for these differences, one *could* argue that high socio-economic levels yield complex socio-economic institutions which, in turn, allow a greater number of channels for political involvement; such seems to be the case with Braşov county. In Iaşi, conversely, political involvement can be said to have been "delayed" until later ages for many deputies because of that region's relative underdevelopment.

Nevertheless, the idea that politicization processes reach people earlier in more developed/modernized places might be only half of the story here, for we have not yet examined the effect Iaşi's recently increased rate of change may have had on initial political interest or involvement.

58 DEMOCRATIC CENTRALISM IN ROMANIA

I think, therefore, that one should be skeptical that such an independent variable (the level of socio-economic advancement) is necessarily the only predictor of political participation.

Many authors (Deutsch, Lerner, Nie, Powell and Prewitt, Lipset and others) have argued, generally, that political participation grows when the socio-economic *level* is higher, even though specific components of that position vary. Yet, data available here indicate that, for Iași—a region where socio-economic levels are *lower*—a higher rate of entry into public life is evident during recent periods. Such an inference can be made since, while the mean and median ages of deputy samples are approximately the same county to county (see Appendix C), many more Iași deputies said that their first political involvement occurred at a mature age. Precisely *why* this apparent "rush" to public life could have taken place in Iași in recent years (i.e., the 1960s) is intriguing.

Perhaps questionnaire responses result from more successful Party co-optation in the Iași area—co-optation being, inherently, a process directed at older, "needed" people with skills and developed expertise. But, Iași's larger proportion of deputies with a later start to their active involvement in public life might also be attributable to that county's higher rate of change from a lower socio-economic level. Any definitive interpretation, however, is especially difficult because participation in a closed political system usually is not based upon a clear-cut individual choice; a deputy in Romania might *not* have decided independently if or when to be politically active, or where and how activities on behalf of the Party are performed.[88]

One potential intervening variable can be eliminated. We know that the Iași population did not suddenly develop a "sense of involvement" in the last decade from seeing decision-makers in action. Romania and other communist-party states have, obviously, continued to be too autocratic for a major opening of policy-making to public view.

We can, moreover, be assured that the differences among counties regarding Question Nine are not a function of another variable, i.e., that the sample from one county is older or younger than the sample from another county. This would have been indicated if, for example, an unexpectedly large part of the Brașov sample were very young (in their 20s), such that initial political experiences necessarily occurred in adolescence. This is not the case, however. Indeed, the four counties' samples

People's Council   59

are *not* significantly different from one another with respect to occupation, age, or sex distribution (P > .10 in all cases). Only with respect
to nationality does a significant difference exist (as expected) among
the four samples (P < .0001). Additionally, one cannot assume that
political involvement comes to people later in relatively rural areas (such
as Iași) because of less "inclination" to participate. Research in Western
Europe has found peasants to participate in politics, in some respects,
as much if not more than their urban counterparts.[89]

There has been, on the other hand, a relative and absolute increase
in living standards in Iași County (noted in Chapter II), corresponding
to an emergence of increasingly active non-political organizations seeking
to influence public life—which will be suggested later in this Section
when considering responses to Question Twenty. Both these developments correspond to Nie, Powell and Prewitt findings.[90] We cannot,
therefore, decide whether a county's socio-economic level or rate of
modernization and development holds the "key" to explain findings
thus far mentioned. Yet, at least coincidentally, this evidence suggests
that the political goals set by the Romanian Communist Party for mod-
ernization/development meant expanded political involvement, planned
or unintentional, for those areas where such socio-economic change
would be relatively greatest (i.e., where either the *pace* of change would
be highest or the amount of change is relatively the most).

This is not to say, of course, that political participation "grows," in
the sense of Western democracies. Indeed, the influence of "public opinion," interests groups, etc., might be siphoned off through a process of
co-optation into the political system, the net result of which could be a
decline in influence.[91]

Open-ended answers were also solicited regarding the beginning of
deputies' political involvement. In Timiș, the great majority referred to
their first political interest and involvement in terms of their career or
place of work—that is, that an interest in public welfare prompted their
awareness of a need for political activity—with fewer responses men-
tioning student experiences, personal motivations, neighborhood requests, etc.

In the city of Cluj, most deputies with whom I spoke mentioned the
20-30 age group as the period for their initial interest in political life.
Although the circumstances surrounding that first active involvement

60   DEMOCRATIC CENTRALISM IN ROMANIA

varied considerably, comments I recorded contained a certain theme:

> ...since I first worked in the factory and recognized the needs of my fellow workers.

> ...as a woman, I saw the need for a strong women's movement in 1945, and became an activist.

> ...because of my work with young people [as an athletic coach] I came into contact with educational problems....It was a very difficult period that needed serious efforts....I felt obligated as a citizen to do more than vote.

> ...until 1948 I was a prisoner of the Russians....I had time to see that no citizen should take his citizenship lightly.

> ...even as a pupil [in high school] I was active in the UTC as a volunteer, as I realized the Party could do most for our country.

Deputies at the county level tended to give this type of response too—that a concern for public welfare created a *"need"* for their activity—which is not altogether different from what an American politician might answer if asked why he had become a candidate for public office.

In communes of Cluj county, however, many deputies seemed unclear as to the circumstances of their first political activity, except in the case of teachers who related their career to obvious public commitment. There were no answers indicating adolescent political interest/involvement in communal Cluj, which tentatively indicates a later arrival of communist-party political institutions in rural areas. Despite a lack of responses in the adolescent category, however, there was no clear consensus among communal deputies in Cluj as to how they became involved, over half of them asserting that there was no reason in particular.

The pattern evident in Cluj was strengthened by the general nature of unstructured responses to Question Nine in Braşov county; namely, that in urban areas, a motivation of "need" for political activity was usually cited, whereas in rural areas this rationale was rarely mentioned. As was the case in Cluj, few rural deputies gave a clear-cut answer as to how it was that they became interested in public life at the age they had indicated.

People's Councils   61

In Iași county, by contrast, a significant proportion (about fifty percent) of county deputies from rural locations and communal deputies evinced alleged motivation from "public need" for their initial political interest/involvement—almost as much as the urban sample.

This difference among counties is not easily explained. Superficially, my conversation with deputies indicated that in Brașov and Cluj counties (and probably Timiș), urban-based deputies were thoroughly "socialized"; either their interest/involvement in local politics truly stemmed from a greater public-mindedness or their answers were modified for my benefit to reflect what they thought the motives for a deputy's political involvement ought to have been. In either case, the term "socialization" seems to cover the possibilities. In Iași, however, deputies are either more uniformly socialized (to include many rural deputies as well) or else there is genuinely a wider concern among deputies for public needs. Because of Iași's lower socio-economic levels, I am led to doubt the former, which leaves us with the real possibility that deputies in Iași county did enter public life for the latter motive.

My probe into the background experiences of people's councils deputies continued in Question Ten asking: "Are you a member of the Romanian Communist Party?" Again, I used a response-keyed procedure whereby if the subject answered "yes," I would ask when he or she had become a party member.

There are several noteworthy patterns in responses to this item. First, it is apparent that very few people who are deputies today joined the Party between 1950 and 1954. This is, historically, a logical finding. Gheorghiu-Dej's purges of postwar members were closely related to his victory over the "muscovite" faction. These purges of 1950 slowed the Party's recruitment during the following period through an insistence that all new members have certain social origins—namely, that of a proletarian, not a bourgeois or an aristocratic background.[92] It is also clear that deputies with party membership dating from the decade between 1955 and 1965 probably constituted the majority of people's councils in three of the four researched counties in 1973 and a plurality in the exception—Brașov.

In other respects, however, responses to Question Ten revealed some significant differences among the four counties. A simplified way to present the nature of such differences is to separate the various five-year

62   DEMOCRATIC CENTRALISM IN ROMANIA

periods into two general categories—"recent" and "not recent." For the
moment, then, we can think of the "before 1945," 1945 through 1949,"
and "1950 through 1954" as "not recent," and the remaining periods
as "recent." Putting Question Ten data into such a configuration reveals
more clearly, I think, the considerable diversity among counties (see
Table XI).

The magnitude of the difference between Iași and Brașov results
tends to suggest agreement with Question Nine responses—that is, an
earlier politicization of deputies in Brașov corresponds with a smaller
percentage of recently-joined party members in the sample. Likewise,
an apparent *later* politicization in Iași corresponds with a higher percentage of more recently-joined party members among deputies interviewed.

There is more to the data here, however, than indicated above. In Iași
County, for instance, where over eighty percent of interviewed deputies
(weighted sample) told of joining the Party after 1954, a correspondingly
high percentage of young deputies does not exist. This, necessarily, means
that a higher percentage of older deputies in Iași are "recent" party
joiners than in Brașov, Cluj or Timiș. An example explains this situation
in another way; if the subject in an interview were a fifty-year-old deputy
in Brașov County, a researcher could assume more confidently that the
deputy had joined the Party before 1955 than if he were interviewing in
Iași County, where many more deputies of that age have recently joined
the Party (as compared with their Brașov counterparts).

In that regard, the similarity between Timiș and Cluj is, again, striking.
Neither county deviates from the other by more than a few percentage
points in any category along the continuum of party membership dates,
save for the "before 1945" and "post 1970" periods. In those latter cases,
it appears that there is less dispersion of party membership dates in Timiș
than in Cluj.

Both questions about the political backgrounds of deputies (Nine and
Ten) have thus far offered an indication of a "pattern" that, while not
firmly established, has an obvious implication; political life in Romania
is *not* uniform. As we have inferred from deputies' responses, neither
initial political interest in an active sense nor entrance into the Communist
Party occur similarly from county to county in Romania. Furthermore,
the manner in which diversity occurs is coincident with the comparative
levels of development/modernization discovered in Chapter II.

TABLE XI

Question Ten: Party Membership Dates

Category of Answer	N = 36 Timiş % (weighted)	N = 45 Cluj % (weighted)	N = 48 Braşov % (weighted)	N = 63 Iaşi % (weighted)
Before 1945	1.1	5.8	1.5	.2
45 thru 49	20.0	16.5	27.9	7.8
50 thru 54	8.1	5.3	4.6	4.3
55 thru 59	25.3	28.6	31.6	24.8
60 thru 64	27.5	23.8	14.8	30.5
65 thru 69	17.4	15.4	17.4	21.1
70—	.6	4.6	2.3	11.2
Total % *not* "recent"	29.2	27.7	34.0	12.4
Total % "recent"	70.8	72.3	66.0	87.6

Note: Non-party responses excluded.

n = 192

(.05 > = > .01)

With answers dichotomized recent/not recent

64   DEMOCRATIC CENTRALISM IN ROMANIA

At this point, however, we need to know more about deputies' background experiences that reflect on the importance of the Party and/or
its front organizations in their political life prior to being elected. Since
this study's purpose is to explore the relationship between socio-economic
and political changes, particularly as posited by a dialectic approach, the
relative position of party activities is important. If deputies cite the Party
less frequently in comparison with other public-political activities before
being elected, this may be one effect of dialectical processes.

An eleventh question, then, asked: "What other activities have you
performed in public life before you were elected as a deputy?" Here, I
wanted deputies to recall their principal earlier public-political activities.
My interest was not in what deputies had done, per se, but rather under
whose auspices public-political actions had been performed. The phrase
"public life" as opposed to "political life" was used in this question to,
first, avoid connotations of party activity that might have narrowed the
scope of deputies' replies, cancelling out their consideration of other non-
party experiences about which I wanted information. Second, the manner
in which individual deputies answered such an inquiry gives an indication
of their own interpretation of the phrase "public life," a factor which will
be discussed shortly.

It became evident that responses could be classified despite their unstructured nature. These categories were as follows:

    I.   Party-U.T.C.
   II.   Front organizations
  III. Non-volunteer, career-related
  IV. Quasi-volunteer
   V. Volunteer
  VI. Student or women's organizations
 VII. None
VIII. Other

The Communist Party and the Union of Communist Youth (Uniunea
Tineretului Comunist or U.T.C.) seemed to coalesce. If the U.T.C. had
been a principal form of public-political involvement mentioned, for
instance, the Party was usually cited in the same breath, or vice versa.

People's Councils 65

Indeed, this as it should be because since the Tenth Party Congress in 1969, party membership has been contingent on prior U.T.C. participation.

The Party-U.T.C. category can and must be differentiated from its primary "front" organizations. Moreover, such subsidiary bodies cannot be classified together. The Sindicat, or General Union of Trade Unions by its more formal title (Uniunea Generala a Sindicatelor din Romania), and the S.U.F. are both mass organizations, for example, of a nature that makes them integral parts of the Party's rule, and almost universal in their membership. While I have previously described the Socialist Unity Front (Section B of this chapter), it should be mentioned here that the Sindicat is, in effect, a nation-wide trade union, encompassing workers of all types—factory or office, white-collar or blue-collar. As the S.U.F. is meant to amalgamate all of Romania's mass organizations, its largest component is the Sindicat, in which there are almost five million members (between a fifth and a quarter of the Romanian population).

Romania's National Council of Women and Union of Student Associations are also part of the network of party-related mechanisms. Nevertheless, in terms of their membership, they are smaller. Furthermore, neither the Council of Women nor the Student Association have direct ministerial representation in Bucharest, like the Sindicat and the U.T.C. Therefore, a separate category was needed for responses indicating activities of these types.

Many deputies responded to Question Eleven by citing a non-volunteer, career-related involvement as their principal contact with public life prior to being elected. This category covered a wide span of answers to include functionaries in the state bureaucracy, teachers, doctors, lawyers, etc.

"Quasi-volunteer" involvement in public life was also cited, which includes such activities as patriotic work and participation in citizens' committees for a street or apartment building. The first of these two answers, patriotic work, refers to labor batallions recruited at one's place of work or residential area for such purposes as construction, harvesting, and the like. Volunteer activities, as such, do exist of course; involvement of this sort, as in the Red Cross, is considered as another classification.

Particularly in these latter three instances, *public* rather than *political* activity is stressed by the respondents. Either the subjects who gave such

66 DEMOCRATIC CENTRALISM IN ROMANIA

answers had no prior activity of a political nature or else they wished to conceal the nature of that involvement. Such an interpretation of the question implies that deputies differentiate between mass organizational membership (as political) and individual action in the public sphere. The latter can occur as part of one's career, by volunteering, or through some type of virtually mandatory participation.

Finally, many subjects answered that they had had no public-political activity prior to becoming a deputy, while a significant number gave "other" responses—the military, avocational-cultural associations, or professional organizations comprising the latter category.

Table XII presents responses to Question Eleven. These data are important in several respects for this study. The Iași responses in Categories I and II indicate that a very small percentage of that county's deputies regard the Party or its primary front organizations as a principal activity before being elected. In a finding with related implications, a very large percentage of Iași deputies said that they had *no* prior public-political experiences before being elected (Category VII). In these same categories, Brașov deputies gave the opposite responses: that is, Brașov has the largest combined percentage for Categories I and II among the four counties, and the lowest percentage for Category VII.

Some qualifications make this result less perfectly dichotomous. In this case, for instance, Brașov County was exceeded slightly by Cluj to the extent to which deputies cited the Party per se as an activity prior to being elected. Brașov, however, totals more than Cluj by a relatively small margin when front organization percentages (from Category II) are combined with prior party experiences.

Iași was also the county where the highest percentages were scored in Categories III and V (career-related and volunteer, respectively). Brașov, meanwhile, scored lowest in both. If it is true that Iași deputies volunteered for public-serving activities and participated in public-related activities through careers *more* than deputies in other counties, then the tentative inference made from unstructured responses to Question Nine may be supported here. That inference was that Iași deputies more often than in other researched counties enter political life out of "concern" for public "needs." At the least, Iași's lead in these two response categories suggests an entry into political life through channels not dependent on mobilization by the Party or its organizational agents.

TABLE XII

Question Eleven: Deputies' Prior Public-Political Activities

Category of Answer	N = 37 Timiș % (weighted)	N = 47 Cluj % (weighted)	N = 50 Brașov % (weighted)	N = 64 Iași % (weighted)
I	28.0	42.2	36.7	9.4
II	10.1	8.7	22.8	5.9
III	15.6	20.0	13.5	20.0
IV	7.5	5.8	10.5	2.0
V	1.1	.4	–	7.9
VI	17.3	2.4	3.1	1.2
VII	11.2	15.2	10.9	45.1
VIII	9.2	5.4	2.4	8.6
Totals	100.0	100.1	99.9	100.1

I – Party-U.T.C.
II – Front Organizations
III – Non-volunteer, career-related
IV – Quasi-volunteer
V – Volunteer
VI – Student or women's organization
VII – None
VIII – Other

N = 198
(P = .0001)

68 DEMOCRATIC CENTRALISM IN ROMANIA

Brașov scored highest in what I have called the "quasi-volunteer category (IV). From responses in this classification, one can detect some indication of the degree to which each county's deputies have been brought into public life through mobilization techniques—a higher percentage suggesting a greater presence of mobilization efforts. Involvement in patriotic work brigades is, perhaps, the most blatant form of "mobilization," although participating in citizens' committees is not entirely by one's own volition either. In both cases, social pressures and a personal "cost-benefit analysis" usually dictate nominal participation. Timiș and Cluj counties both scored higher in this regard than did Iași, but neither exceeded Brașov County.

Timiș County's unexpectedly large score in the "student and women's organization" category (VI) is not easily explained. Partly responsible could be a significantly better organized women's association in Timiș. The magnitude of difference among counties in the sixth category of responses, however, clearly exceeds the explanatory power of this factor alone.

Finally, in the general category (VIII), there seems to be a similarity among counties with the exception of Brașov, which has the smallest percentage. Within Brașov, then, there appears to be less diversity of activities in the public sphere prior to becoming a deputy.

These data point, once again, to sub-national political diversity in Romania. In this case, the extent to which the Party and its front organizations were part of deputies' activities before being elected *increases* as a county's development/modernization increase.

Our final concern in this section of Chapter IV is the questionnaire's fourteenth item, which asked: "Are you a member of the following organizations. . ," and then listed possible answers.[93] My intention was to obtain a comparative measure of how active people's council deputies are during their tenure in that position. This item produced a quantitative measure so that each deputy could be rated on the following scale:

Category	No. of Organizations Mentioned
very active	4+
moderately active	3
nominally active	2
minimally active	1
inactive	0

People's Councils   69

Such a scale, of course, lacks qualitative indices. For example, belonging to the Sindicat does not indicate the extent of one's involvement. Indeed, a deputy could be extremely active in the Sindicat and nothing else, yet be rated lower in the foregoing scale than another deputy who, nominally at least, is a member of two or three organizations. Recognizing this, I attempted to gain another measure of the degree of participation in Question Fifteen: "How have you participated in one or more the organizations previously mentioned (listed above)—always, occasionally, or never?" This inquiry, however, met with unenlightening results. Deputies, almost without exception, answered that they "always" participated in such organizations where they held membership. Therefore, we are left with a one-dimensional picture of deputies' present outside activites.

There are several principal conclusions that one might make from these data. First, a simplified restatement of weighted responses to Question Fourteen (in Figure II) indicates that over one-quarter of deputies in Iași County are "above average" in the number of non-party organizations to which they belong, whereas only 18% of Brașov deputies are as involved. Second, Brașov has a slightly larger percentage of deputies relative to other researched counties who are "nominally involved," i.e., having two non-party organizational memberships. Third, *both* Iași and Brașov counties have proportionately fewer deputies than either Cluj or Timiș who are only involved minimally or not at all, and therefore below average in their non-party organizational membership.

Here, one discovers that "above average" non-party organizational involvement does *not* increase among deputies as the level of a county's development/modernization increases—as one might have otherwise expected. (The data are not, however, significant at a level $\leqslant .05$, which means that we cannot confidently accept these findings.) Indeed, there is somewhat an inverse tendency. Iași County, with the lowest socio-economic level of the four researched districts, has both the highest "above average" score of organizational membership *and* the lowest "below average" score. Taken together, these scores imply an overall non-party involvement greater among Iași deputies than in the other three counties. This information supports inferences made earlier (from Question Eleven), where it was suggested that comparatively few Iași deputies recalled the Party or its front organizations as principal activities before becoming council members. Furthermore, Brașov County's responses to Question

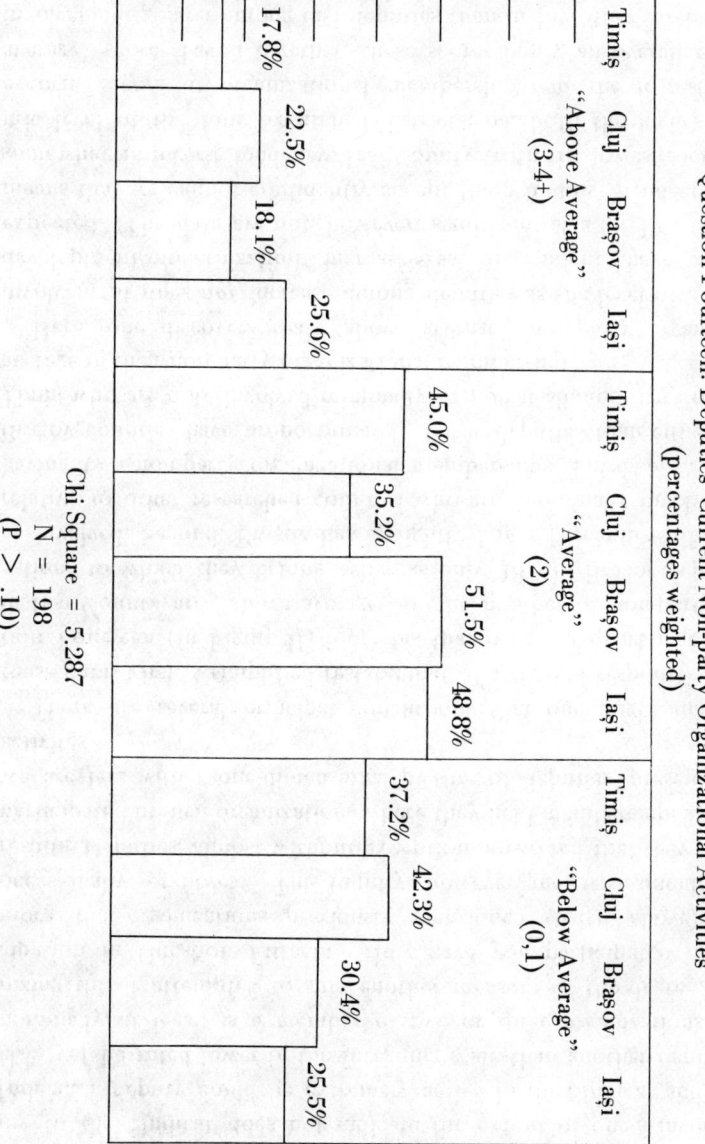

FIGURE II
Question Fourteen: Deputies' Current Non-party Organizational Activities
(percentages weighted)

Chi Square = 5.287
N = 198
(P > .10)

People's Councils 71

Fourteen were unexpected—if, that is, one's expectations were based on responses from each of the previous questions (Nine through Eleven). Braşov, indeed, might have been the most likely candidate for the scores that we find Iaşi to have achieved on the last item (Fourteen).

Because these data measured the extent of *non-party* organizational membership among deputies, it is particularly important for this study that Iaşi should be found leading the other three counties. Iaşi's higher non-party activity among deputies may constitute evidence that a greater rate of socio-economic change is inversely related with party-dominated political life. One cannot say with assurance that rapid modernization/development promote organizational activity outside the Communist Party in Romania, but we can say that these two phenomena seem co-incident. Coincident as they are, then, it is possible that more rapid socio-economic change fosters (and, indeed, necessitates) social mobilization and group consciousness before the Party has succeeded in establishing its own channels for activity.[94]

It is not a new notion, of course, that "rapid growth" increases the propensity for group organization in a social system.[95] Yet, if deputies join *more* groups outside the Party in a rapidly changing locality than elsewhere, this information could put a new "twist" to an old idea—specifically, a dialectical "twist." The development and modernization sought by the Party might, then, promote deputies' activities away from the Party in places where socio-economic change is relatively most rapid.

The constrast provided by these last responses illuminates a distinction suggested earlier in this study—between what a socio-economic *level* might connote for political life as opposed to a *rate* of socio-economic change. Answers to Questions Nine through Eleven of the questionnaire are, in general, mutually supportive. Together they suggest a direct relationship between such qualities as active interest or involvement in politics, party membership dates, and prior public/political activities and the level of development/moderniztion. Data generated by Question Fourteen, on the one hand, point to a relationship between the rate of socio-economic change and non-party organizational membership.

More specifically, Questions Nine through Fourteen have tended to suggest that

1) deputies became actively interested or involved in politics earliest in Braşov, latest in Iaşi, and somewhat earlier in Timiş than in Cluj (from Question Nine);

72   DEMOCRATIC CENTRALISM IN ROMANIA

2) deputies in Brașov joined the Party least recently and in Iași most
   recently, while Timiș deputies joined later than Brașov, but earlier
   than Cluj (from Question Ten);

3) public-political activities prior to becoming a deputy are most
   closely associated with the Party in Brașov and least in Iași, while
   Cluj ranks ahead of Timiș in this case (from Question Eleven);

4) the extent of current non-party organizational membership among
   deputies is greatest in Iași, whereas Brașov deputies rank ahead of
   Timiș but behind Cluj (from Question Fourteen).

The first two of these points indicate two sides of a single phenomenon
—namely, that politicization occurs earliest in the most developed/modern-
ized county and that such politicization corresponds to early party membership. The Party and its front organizations, therefore, might be expected
to be most pervasive in Brașov and least so in Iași. Indeed, responses to
Question Eleven seemed to confirm that suspicion.

Yet, deputies in Iași are more active outside the Party than their
counterparts in other counties according to the weighted sample data.
Because Iași, as a less developed/modernized area of Romania, would
likely have fewer channels for such involvement, such an indication of
greater non-party activity there is intriguing. One is led to suspect that it
is not *in spite of* its under-development but *because of* its rate of change
that Iași County deputies are members of more organizations outside the
Party than deputies in other, more "advanced" regions of Romania.

With these insights into deputies' backgrounds, we can now turn to
data regarding their opinions and concerns. Background information has
hinted at dialectical relationships and has portrayed the nature of political diversity within Romania. In Section D, a wide range of deputies'
political opinions are examined for other indicators.

D: DEPUTIES' OPINIONS

Questions Sixteen and Seventeen focus upon the opinions of people's
council deputies by asking about the problems confronting their People's
Council. This and following items on the questionnaire were intended to

People's Councils 73

gain evidence bearing directly on the potential relevance of a dialectic approach. I was, then, interested not only in the qualitative diversity of problems among counties but also in the extent to which, in one county, matters of public concern are more prevalent than in another.

For Question Sixteen, unlike previous questions, there was no attempt to structure responses. I wanted to gain an approximate measure of how many "problems" existed in the deputies' opinions. Because of this intention, I did not limit the number of problems mentioned or try to isolate responses in preconceived categories. The mean number of problems mentioned, therefore, offers a comparative gauge among the four counties as to the quantity of local problems or the extent to which deputies recognize tasks facing their local government.

Actual deputy responses were distributed as follows:

Level	Location			
	Timiş	Cluj	Braşov	Iaşi
Town-City	68	39	59	60
County	7	36	42	51
Commune	22	22	16	60

In other words, to the extent that I was able to separate distinct "problems" or "issues" within the unstructured replies of deputies, 23 deputies from Timiş towns and cities mentioned a total of 68 "problems" for their council in the next one to three years.

For each level of each county, a mean number of responses per deputy can be calculated. The resulting scores are, quite simply, the "average" number of "problems" mentioned by deputies from the locale and level indicated in the sample. From these means one might infer that certain levels or areas do have more problems—or, at least, that deputies have that opinion.

Level	Location			
	Timiş	Cluj	Braşov	Iaşi
Town-City	2.96	2.29	2.68	3.00
County	2.33	3.00	2.10	2.68
Commune	2.00	1.22	2.00	2.40

74   DEMOCRATIC CENTRALISM IN ROMANIA

Knowing such "averages" per deputy of each locale and level, it is possible to correct for location biases in the sample. After weighting, responses were redistributed as follows:

Level	Location			
	Timiș	Cluj	Brașov	Iași
Town-City	14.21	15.38	30.66	14.40
County	3.80	6.34	6.93	7.19
Commune	61.16	46.56	70.50	135.60
Total Responses	79.19	68.26	108.09	157.18
Mean Responses Per Deputy (weighted)	2.14	1.46	2.16	2.46

In some respects, the raw averages for each level, as well as the weighted means above, represented expected results. One finds, for instance, that commune-level deputies consistently mentioned fewer problems than county or city-level council members. Furthermore, with the exception of Cluj, city deputies mentioned more problems than county deputies. Yet, it would be inappropriate to conclude immediately from such results that there are more problems in cities for local political institutions than in rural areas (although one might suspect that such is the case). Mean scores of the sort indicated *could* have been produced by a difference in the "awareness" among deputies regarding local concerns and problems; that is, city deputies might mention more problems simply because they are knowledgeable about a greater number. If that were so, however, the least urbanized county (Iași) should have lower mean scores, which it does not. Quite the contrary, the location with the lowest socio-economic level and smallest urban population has, overall, the highest grand mean score, denoting more problems mentioned by deputies on the average.

The strong suspicion arises, then, that a region such as Iași County, experiencing socio-economic change more rapidly than the other counties, does indeed have more problems that are recognized by people's council deputies. Moreover, it is significant that deputies from Iași County consistently mentioned more concerns for their people's councils than did Brașov deputies, regardless of location.

The findings must be seen in conjunction with the information gained from earlier questionnaire items which suggest that political backgrounds

People's Councils

of deputies are diverse in ways coincident with socio-economic levels and/or rates of change of their respective counties. If, for instance, Iaşi deputies mention more concerns for their councils neither because of, nor despite a different socio-economic level, but due to that region's more rapid transformation from a low socio-economic level, then a dialectic approach could appear plausible. In fact, as noted regarding Question Sixteen, it is *not* merely that urban deputies see more problems for their councils. More significantly, Iaşi deputies, *irrespective* of where they come from within that county, tend to indicate more concerns than their counterparts elsewhere. One can only conclude, then, that there is something peculiar to Iaşi which fosters such a result, not differences between urban and rural deputies.

Another kind of measure is needed, however, of deputies' opinions regarding local problems—a measure based on limited responses. In Question Seventeen (see Table XIII) I sought to have deputies identify the *most* pressing single concern for the people's council to which they belong. Taken together, data from the four counties produced by Question Seventeen give an interesting portrait of concerns for sub-national political institutions in a developing communist party state. For the most part, common-sense assessments about what developing states face are reconfirmed.

Agriculture is a major preoccupation of the deputies from all counties. In a nation where half the population is peasantry, this should surprise no one. That Braşov deputies are less concerned with agriculture relative to other problems (even at the commune level) is also to be expected, given that district's higher socio-economic level. Yet, for much of Romania, agriculture *is* daily life and cannot be disassociated from the concerns of people's councils, irrespective of any desire to work for "industry," "urbanization," and other panaceas. As one Iaşi commune-level deputy told me: "Our major concern has always been and will always be agriculture; the fields are our lives."[96]

Industry and industrialization are the province of urban-based deputies. Yet, given the great emphasis on increasing industrial production in Romania, the responses were surprisingly few. The economic "plan" is an omnipresent goal in Romania if one believes innumerable party announcements, decrees, etc., the achievement of which is always held up as a solution to whatever ails the country. A Five-Year Plan must not only be achieved, but a massive campaign urges each enterprise and individual

TABLE XIII

Question Seventeen: Deputies' Opinions of Most Important Problem for People's Council

Category of Response	N = 37 Timiş % (weighted)	N = 47 Cluj % (weighted)	N = 198 Braşov % (weighted)	N = 50 Braşov % (weighted)	N = 64 Iaşi % (weighted)
Economic[1]	30.6	15.2		11.8	19.9
Quality of Life[2]	28.1	47.5		34.1	33.8
Education	40.7	17.8		21.1	23.3
General Development/ Modernization[3]	0	19.1		29.2	22.2
Other[4]	.6	.4		3.8	.8
Totals	100.0%	100.0%	100.0%	100.0%	100.0%

$(.05 \geq = P - > .01)$

1. "Economic" answers included those focused on agriculture or industry.
2. "Quality of Life" answers included those focused on public services, housing, provisioning, health and sanitation, roads and transportation, and urban planning.
3. "General Development/Modernization" answers were those which utilized such terms without offering a specific substantive area.
4. "Other" includes finance, parks, democratization, day care centers, etc.

People's Councils 77

worker to complete the Plan before schedule.[97] It is interesting, then, that local deputies are so little oriented toward the industrial aspects of "multi-lateral development" sought by central authorities.

Scores in the "education" category indicate, rather convincingly, that this area of concern in very important. In all cases, education ranks third or higher among all categories in terms of the percentage of deputies citing it as the problem for primary council concern (in Timiş, it was first). Components of this concern centered around expanding minimum education to the entire population—specifically, to the ten years now required as opposed to the previous minimum of eight grades. Material conditions of the schools—sufficient classrooms, books, etc.—were also part of the education "problem." In urban areas, the principal educational concern was material in nature, i.e., improving the quality of education. By contrast, rural deputies' primary concern was reaching the ten-grade required level. Because Iaşi County has fewer young people who continue on to the higher secondary grades (see Chapter II), the latter answer was more prevalent there than in the other counties and, particularly, relative to Braşov.

Provisioning and other "quality of life" indicators continue to pose a problem, or at least an irritant, in Romania, as in other socialist countries, not so much because of actual product shortages as because of poor distribution. In the city of Cluj, for instance, a number of deputies mentioned consumer products, generally, as a problem for their council, arguing that they personally knew of certain villages where items, in short supply in Cluj, were plentiful. Particularly traumatic, apparently, was the lack of beer (in a hot August), most of which was on the Black Sea coast, destined for German and Italian tourists. Iaşi deputies and rural deputies generally indicated less concern for the supply of food and consumer items, whereas urban-based deputies tended to be more vocal in this regard.

Housing and construction appeared as a major concern in Braşov more than elsewhere, subsumed under the category of "quality of life." A Braşov city deputy noted that "thirty percent of the town is a big construction site," and another lamented that the completion of new "blocs" (Romanian spelling) of apartments was not yet in view.[98] The impatience underlying those statements contrasted with a commune-level Iaşi deputy who observed that, "compared with twenty years ago, our homes are like

DEMOCRATIC CENTRALISM IN ROMANIA

villas today."[99] Overall, 26% of the Braşov sample (weighted) and only 5% of the Iaşi deputies (weighted) cited housing as a problem needing attention by the people's council.

Several factors could account for the dictotomy between answers given by Iaşi and Braşov deputies. First, although Iaşi county is, overall, more densely populated, Braşov's population is more confined to towns and cities; even the mountainous topography of Braşov promotes the concentration of population. One can, then, speculate that the opinions of deputies mirror the concerns of a more highly concentrated (i.e., more often urban) populace for housing and construction quality.

Other reasons for the above-mentioned responses seem feasible as well. It may be, for instance, that subjective "trade-offs" are involved for Braşov county citizens by living in an area more developed/modernized. Life is clearly better in a material sense in contrast to, say, Iaşi, but so too do inconveniences related to that higher standard of living seem larger. Perhaps a better way of putting this notion is that Braşov citizens may expect comforts, having had them longer, and therefore be relatively more irritated when construction is not completed or when an apartment's facilities do not work. Iaşi citizens, by contrast, may be only too happy to see construction taking place, and may be more tolerant of inoperative features in buildings that were new to them anyway.

General development and modernization, which I used as a "catch-all" category here, was of universal concern. That Timiş County has no score in that category resulted from my attempt, in the early stages of research, to seek specific responses from all deputies.

In all of this, there is little to shake one's prior intuitive assessments. For our purposes, however, the thesis of intra-national diversity of opinions (i.e., not just backgrounds) about public policy is again supported and, here, portrayed with greater clarity. The most important conclusion that can be made is that deputies tend to be most concerned with day-to-day problems peculiar to their local area, *not*, it would seem, with broadly-based national goals (e.g., of industrialization, social democracy, etc.) Instead, varying from area to area as one would expect, deputies' concerns reflect immediacy and a certain mundane quality—finishing housing and construction, assuring basic food and consumer supplies, having good roads and trams, and educating their children. If deputies to Romanian

People's Councils 79

people's councils are aware of party-decreed aims such as a "multilaterally developed socialist society" it must be a distinctly secondary awareness.

We can accept with some confidence (because these data are statistically significant) the idea that opinions are diverse among deputies, and that locally-based problems tend to take precedence in deputies' minds over nation-wide goals promoted by the party. Regarding the dialectic approach, however, we need to find whether or not specifically political opinions of deputies vary county to county in any way corresponding to socio-economic differences. To that end, the questionnaire's eighteenth item asked deputies what changes they thought were needed to improve the council of which they were members.

Responses (Table XIV) imply that Iași County has fewer deputies who say that no changes (or no improvements) are needed in their council, whereas Brașov County has, proportionately, the most deputies who indicate total satisfaction with their council.

More important are the types of improvements suggested. In administering the questionnaire, structured responses were listed first, and then an opportunity for unstructured answers was offered. The five structured replies are relatively innocuous for communist-party politics and are classified as "intra-systemic." Among open-ended responses, several clusters became evident:

1) give deputies and the people's council more power, more important work, or more responsibility;

2) improve the quality of deputies, i.e., better preparation, more education or better attitudes towards their work;

3) enlarge citizen involvement and participation;

4) improve expertise and competence of bureaucracy;

5) increase the number of candidates in each district;

6) improve local leadership.

Each of these responses, quite clearly, implies a greater dissatisfaction with the system of local politics, and they are thus classified as "extra-systemic."

TABLE XIV

Question Eighteen: Changes Needed in People's Councils According to Deputies

Category of Answer	N = 37 Timiș % (weighted)	N = 47 Cluj % (weighted)	N = 50 Brașov % (weighted)	N = 64 Iași % (weighted)
No Changes Needed	28.0	39.4	44.5	19.4
Changes, Intra-Systemic[1]	64.0	25.0	33.8	28.7
Changes, Extra-Systemic[2]	8.1	35.7	21.7	52.0
Totals	100.1%	100.1%	100.0%	100.0%

N = 198
(P < or = .001)

1. "Intra-systemic" changes include: (a) reduce number of deputies, (b) better preparation for sessions, (c) lengthen sessions, (d) increase number of deputies, (e) improve permanent commission activities.
2. "Extra-systemic" changes include: (a) more power or responsibility to deputies, (b) need better qualified deputies, (c) more citizen involvement, (d) better expertise in administration, (e) more candidates per district and several other responses.

People's Councils   81

There is uniformly little sentiment for measures offered as structured responses such as increasing or decreasing the number of deputies or lengthening sessions. Better preparation for sessions received some support as did suggested improvements in the activities of standing commissions of the people's councils. Particularly in the latter case, it was a common complaint of deputies that recommendations from standing commissions went unheeded—more so in the less developed/modernized counties than in the more "advanced" regions.

When a deputy chose to give an answer other than those verbally listed, a surprising proportion in Iași County and in the city of Cluj indicated that they thought more power and/or responsibilities should be given to deputies and the people's councils generally. Such a proposal connotes, of course, a departure from party-ordained procedures in local politics, and is therefore categorized as "extra-systemic." One Cluj municipal deputy articulated this position better than most:

> Deputies must have a stronger relationship with the executive committee, and have more influence with it. As it is now, we deputies just wait around for orders. I think, in my personal opinion, that we need to initiate things, not only respond.[100]

In Iași, some deputies called for a greater "delegation of authority" to deputies and the council from the permanent bureau and executive committee. Other subjects were more explicit:

> Deputies cannot arrange anything now; if the people ask deputies to do anything, we must plead with the executive committee. Deputies need more authority. For example, we should be able to deal directly with pollution from a factory rather than go through the executive committee. Deputies should not just be intermediaries.[101]

More succinctly, another Iași deputy said that there was "not much of importance" done in the people's council.

Despite these interesting statments, one must recall that relatively few deputies openly expressed thoughts contrary to the established mode of local politics, whether or not they might have agreed with the general sentiments. Only in Iași did a bare majority favor significant changes in local politics.

82   DEMOCRATIC CENTRALISM IN ROMANIA

Critical of their compatriots, a number of deputies suggested that people's councils could be improved if people elected as deputies were of higher quality. Specific references were made to (1) the need for higher educational levels and (2) the necessity of committed attitudes on the part of council members. At least some of the responses in this category dealt with other council members in the condescending tone, such as one Cluj deputy who judged some of his fellow deputies as "not too bright"; as he continued, the deputy noted that among over 200 deputies in his his council, "some do not know much now."[102] Other answers placed in this category were of a considerably different sort, asserting that not all deputies practiced a "socialist mentality." Most responses that referred to attitudinal improvements, however, seemed aimed at deputies who are nominal members at best, having little time or inclination to play the role of a deputy outside people's council sessions.

A degree of concern is in evidence in all counties for citizen-people's council relations or contacts. There does not seem to be any significant difference county to county in this regard, however, except insofar as Brașov city deputies register greater concern for citizen involvement in local government than do urban deputies in less developed/modernized counties.

Thus, in the most rapidly changing county, Iași, fewer deputies are satisfied with the people's council or, at least, a higher proportion think that something could be done to improve their council. In addition, we have found that Iași has a relatively higher proportion of deputies who suggest improvements that connote major systemic changes—that is, potentially counter to party-control of local political institutions.

Question Nineteen, in most respects, reconfirmed what other measures of deputies' opinions had detected. Subjects were to reflect upon the accomplishments of their council in response to the question: "What is the most important activity which the people's council performs for the public?" Data are presented in Table XV.

One should not, of course, attribute all these "good deeds" for the public to people's council activities alone, despite the deputies' assertions. Instead of measuring actual accomplishments by people's councils, then, the question sought another way of looking at council members' opinions regarding public policies.

Brașov deputies scored highest (relative to the four counties) in the category of "economics" because many replied that their council's most

TABLE XV

Question Nineteen: Most Important People's Council Activities for the Public in Deputies' Opinions

Category of Answer	N = 37 Timiş % (weighted)	N = 47 Cluj % (weighted)	N = 50 Braşov % (weighted)	N = 64 Iaşi % (weighted)
Economic[1]	17.6	14.4	22.6	18.9
Education[2]	15.0	18.9	.8	5.6
Quality of Life	57.6	51.6	62.5	52.3
General Development/ Modernization	9.2	9.4	11.2	11.5
Other	.6	5.7	2.9	11.7

N = 198
(P = .10)

1. Includes agriculture and industry.
2. Includes provisioning, housing quality and availability, public service and maintenance, urbanization, and other responses generally connoting a better life and standard of living.

84   DEMOCRATIC CENTRALISM IN ROMANIA

vital activity was in promoting industry. Meanwhile, Iași County's deputies
had a wider dispersion of concerns, i.e., a higher percentage in the categories "education" and "other." These scores translate to mean that
people's council deputies from counties as different as are Brașov and
Iași (in terms of socio-economic levels on the one hand and rates of
change on the other) may see the accomplishments of that local state
organ in somewhat dissimilar ways. Differences are too small, however,
to warrant a confident statement to that effect at this time (P = .10).

As indicated in Table XVI, a relationship seems to be present between
the counties' rates of socio-economic change and answers to Question
Twenty. That is, the more rapidly changing a county is, the higher percent of its deputies who responded affirmatively (i.e., saying that there
are non-political organizations which influence public life). As a corollary,
the higher a county's socio-economic *level*, the greater proportion of
deputies who answered negatively. Such a pattern of responses may be
indicative of more political activity in Iași or that more deputies think
there are greater efforts to influnce public life by non-political organizations. Inferring the above relationship assumes that attempts by non-
political organizations (however the deputies might have conceived that
term) to influence public matters are part of specifically *political* processes
through which one group seeks to effect policies beneficial to them as
opposed to another group. Given such a premise, Brașov County appears
to be, according to this measure, no more politically active than Cluj
or Timiș and less so than Iași, despite its (Brașov's) greater development/
modernization.

In the context of this study's inquiry, Question Twenty data carry an
important message: if modernizing/developmental changes planned by
the Party, promoted by its front organizations and implemented through
state organs have, as one consequence, the increasing presence of ostensibly
non-political organizations which seek to influence public life, *then* a
dialectic approach may be a viable way of viewing such phenomena.
Such an inference can be made because the pace of the Party's modernization and development program seems to be connected antithetically
with its own (the Party's) hegemony over political processes. Differences
among countries are not, however, statistically significant in the sample
of deputies, meaning that these conclusions cannot be made with
confidence.

TABLE XVI

Question Twenty: Presence of Non-Political Organizations Which Influence Public in Deputies' Opinions

Category of Response	N = 37 Timiș % (weighted)	N = 47 Cluj % (weighted)	N = 50 Brașov % (weighted)	N = 64 Iași % (weighted)
Yes	48.1	44.2	43.2	50.9
No	51.9	55.8	56.8	49.1
Totals	100.0%	100.0%	100.0%	100.0%

N = 198
(P > .10)

Deputies who answered affirmatively offered a wide variety of responses when asked *how* non-political organizations made their influence felt. From these unstructured replies, no strong tendencies differentiated one county from another. The means by which such organizations try to influence the implementation of public policy (and to a negligible degree, the making of policy), according to deputies, included "official" channels such as making proposals to a standing commission of the people's councils, going to S.U.F. meetings with requests or complaints, or having a group member who is a deputy bring a matter of group interest directly to a people's council officer (e.g., an executive committee member). Clearly, if a non-political organization is "represented" in the executive committee of a people's council itself, and therefore in the local party hierarchy as well, its interests can be pursued with fewer detours.

It would be a mistake to assume here, however, that associated groups in Romania (aside from the Party and its front organizations) can assert themselves in anything more than the most circumspect of ways. I gained no impression from deputies (even from those answering "yes" to Question Twenty) that professional organizations, sports groups, cultural associations or any other associated group could argue for more resources or different policies in their realm without considerable restraints. Indeed, some deputies' answers involved what may be a realistic assessment—that non-political organizations exist in Romania, but that they have no influence in public life (that is, beyond their own membership).

It seems unlikely that differences between counties on this questionnaire item follow from greater party success at convincing deputies in Iaşi, as opposed to deputies elsewhere, to take democratic propaganda literally. This interpretation would credit deputies of more developed/modernized areas with being somehow more sophisticated and realistic, while attributing to people in less-developed/modernized regions a tendency to accept party teachings rotely.

Yet, one should note that "sophistication" and "realism" are not necessarily derived from high living standards. One could, as easily and as inaccurately, argue that to live simply necessarily means a commitment to "honesty". More substantial grounds exist, however, for rejecting the alternative argument. As related earlier in this chapter, Iaşi deputies were more willing to voice needs for improvements in people's councils (Question Eighteen) and were more active outside the Party (Question Fourteen).

People's Councils   87

There is, then, evidence to suggest that Iași deputies do anything but accept the Party's propaganda literally; clearly, we cannot explain Question Twenty's data by assuming that Iași citizens and deputies are more susceptible to "brainwashing."

Subsuming all socio-economic interests beneath the aegis of the Party or its primary front organizations is, of course, integral to communist party regimes. Where that effort has been most successful, organizations can make inputs into policy-implementation only when participation is asked for or demanded of them by the Party. If deputies' opinions are any indication, then associated groups in Iași, Timiș, and to a degree in Cluj may operate somewhat more "freely" than in Brașov County—that is, there could be less party control as to when and how organizations attempt to be influential outside their own membership (remembering, of course, that this is an entirely relative statement, dealing wiht a closed political system).

The role deputies play in organizations outside the Party was also brought out in unstructured replies to Question Twenty. Many deputies who are members of one or more outside groups, as most are, openly stated that they attempted to gain more money or resources for that group, or to work for laws and/or policies seen by their organizations as preferable. For example, a deputy in Brașov who practiced medicine told of his attempts on behalf of the local medical association to gain new, more stringent sanitation laws. Another deputy, an artist by avocation, sought an exhibition hall for his fellow painters and sculptors, using his position as leverage in the city bureaucracy to procure space. "Deputies work for their friends as well as the public," said one deputy with no reluctance, since his opinion seemed to mirror that of many of his counterparts.[103]

In that regard, a worthwhile digression is appropriate. A vital part of all Romanian politics (and Balkan politics writ large) is a variation of a familiar theme—what can loosely be called "connections" (relații or pile). This is not "corruption" in the prejorative sense of that English term nor as restricted as nepotisim, but akin to clientalism,[104] in that it is a de facto institution probably necessary for maintaining any political regime. Deputies occupy an important place in that system; they, like predecessors in non-socialist regimes, have been co-opted by a pervading societal "way of doing things." Simply put, to get any service done, and

88   DEMOCRATIC CENTRALISM IN ROMANIA

done right, one needs to "know someone"—to "have an in." A deputy is, for many citizens, a means of avoiding bureaucratic tangles, and he (the deputy) therefore becomes a dispenser of favors, and an interlocutor. This does not mean that the individual who is a deputy is "powerful" in his own right for, like the machine politics of American history, a deputy outside the executive committee is much more controlled than empowered (controlled by the Party, the S.U.F., the Sindicat, the U.T.C., and likely a combination).

In daily life, "pile" (or "pull" as used in the common Romanian expression) is manifested, for example, by the need to "tip" (one could say "bribe") repairmen of autos, appliances, shoes, ad infinitum, in order to have a better chance of receiving prompt, careful work. In that sense, some material reward helps create the needed "connection." Deputies, too, receive benefits, although it is less clear that their efforts are effectual. Their rewards, furthermore, are not as blatant as in the example cited, but do occur nevertheless. This subject will be given further consideration shortly.

We have, thus far, seen several indications that, in regions where development/modernization are proceeding faster from relatively lower socioeconomic levels, there seems to be more political life outside the Party. A tentative pattern has begun to emerge in the deputies' opinion that leads one to inquire further.

If dialectics help explain politics in developing/modernizing communist states, then some aspect of the dialectical process should be seen as citizens and regime interact on the local level. One perspective of this interaction can be obtained from participants in the state apparatus, in this case people's council members. Remembering that our source here is deputies' opinions about how the institutions of government and the populace interact (and not a public opinion poll), Question Twenty-one sought unstructured replies by asking, "What are the methods or means used by the people's councils or other local governmental institutions to attract and interest citizens in public life?" (See Table XVII.)

Especially clear in Table XVII are the following tendencies:

1) a much greater reliance on citizens' committees in Brașov and
    Cluj than in Timiș or Iași;

TABLE XVII

Question Twenty-one: Means of Interesting Citizens in Public Life

Category of Answer	N = 37 Timiş % (weighted)	N = 47 Cluj % (weighted)	N = 50 Braşov % (weighted)	N = 64 Iaşi % (weighted)
Citizens' Committees	22.1	45.9	57.1	25.1
Party and Front Organizations	16.4	7.8	6.6	.4
Deputies' Personal Contact	34.5	22.8	21.1	34.9
Patriotic Work	8.4	6.2	.3	9.6
Education and Propaganda	16.9	12.3	12.9	26.0
Other	1.7	4.9	2.1	3.9
Totals	100.0%	99.9%	100.1%	99.9%

N = 198
(.01 = P > .001)

90 DEMOCRATIC CENTRALISM IN ROMANIA

2) a greater reliance on personal duty encounters in Iași and Timiș than in the other two counties;

3) a greater use of patriotic work in Iași and Timiș than in Cluj and Brașov;

4) a greater importance of education in Iași and Timiș than Cluj and, obviously, Brașov.

Such conclusions offer an approximation of how deputies think governmental organs try to interest citizens in public life in their territorial-administrative area. These statements should not be construed such that deputies appear to be saying that there is more patriotic work in Iași and Timiș than in Cluj or Brașov. Instead, the answers suggest only that political institutions go about their business of "mobilization" using different techniques or combination of methods.

Scores for the two most-often mentioned means of interesting citizens in public life (citizens' committees and deputies contacts) are, as one can easily observe, bound to location. In other words, scores do not fluctuate similarily nation-wide; deputies' personal contacts with citizens are not, for instance, the most important method to attract citizens to public life throughout Romania, but only in counties with higher rates of socio-economic change and lower socio-economic levels. Meanwhile, a more "advanced" area with a slower pace of change such as Brașov County scores higher in the category "citizens' committees" (organizations formed around "blocs" of flats and/or city streets).

While these data are significant, some of the other scores in Table XVII are not as neatly dichotomized, since Brașov and Iași do not always appear on opposite sides of a continuum. For example, the Party and its front organization, the S.U.F., were mentioned proportionately more in Timiș than in either Brașov or Iași counties. On the other hand, some scores are more easily explained, as in the case of the "education-propaganda" category, where deputies from the least developed/modernized county (and least educated) regard in-school methods of considerable importance, where Brașov and Cluj deputies less frequently mentioned this means of interesting citizens. Similarly, Iași's "patriotic work" score is higher than Brașov's by such a degree probably due to the greater need (and thus availability) of agricultural work projects (planting, harvesting,

People's Councils   91

hoeing, etc.). This can be contrasted to Braşov's more developed/modern-
ized setting where fewer "make-work" projects are available, and there is
less need for agricultural patriotic work (although, to be sure, students,
the Army and others not occupied with production *do* harvest potatoes,
dig beets, and the like, in Braşov).

Question Twenty-two asked about the manner in which one becomes
a people's council deputy in Romania. In discussions with deputies, I
sought and was able to obtain their opinions as to why they were nominated and how they were informed of their selection. The diverse responses
county to county and even within a single county ran counter to my
general expectations. I had expected that in a unitary communist-party
state, both the reasons for certain people becoming deputies and the
procedures through which their recruitment and election are effected
would be quite consistent.

From questionnaire replies, a tendency was revealed for Brasov deputies
more than other counties, and Cluj and Timiş more than Iaşi, to think
that their Party or front organization activities brought about their nomination. Iaşi had proportionately the most deputies (relative to the other
counties) who indicated that they though their expertise or some specific
skill had gianed the nomination. Meanwhile, both Cluj and Timiş counties'
deputies seemed to lay greater stress on having been a "good worker" or
a "good household manager" (gospodar),[105] as opposed to other types
of responses.

There are many intervening variables, of course, that could bring about
differences among counties other than the dialectics of development/
modernization. Furthermore, one cannot infer that Iaşi deputies are any
less loyal and/or obedient to the Party simply because they more often
think their selection as candidates was due to some demonstrated skill
or knowledge instead of party-related activity. It is, nevertheless, consistent with information suggested earlier in this chapter that intra-national
differences exist among deputies' opinions regarding reasons for their
selection.

When deputies were asked how they found out that they had been
proposed as a candidate, a large majority from all four counties said that
either a delegation or individual from the Socialist Unity Front had
notified them. Naturally, this is only part of the story, since the S.U.F.
provides only a formal notification. Usually deputies-to-be hear from other

sources earlier, depending on their prior status. Almost all are told by other citizens that, at a citizen's committee meeting, his or her name was brought up as a good prospect for deputy from that district. But there are other echelons of deputies, some of whom are sufficiently important to be approached directly by a party official or an officer in the people's council. Braşov County led other counties in this last respect, although very few deputies gave such an answer.

More generally, I wanted to learn if becoming a deputy involved one process or many within Romania. There are, I found, certain formal touchstones through which each deputy-to-be must pass. Nevertheless, considerable differences in the "operational procedures" exist which seemed to be determined by the "importance" of a deputy-to-be.

For want of better terms, one can divide deputies into three groups by virtue of their importance—the local political elite, the "needed" and the "fillers." Very few deputies are members of the permanent bureau of each people's council. Contrary to the People's Council Law of 1968, the permanent bureau and executive committee are not elected in any competitive way from the body of deputies since the former are handed deputies' posts by virtue of their elite status.

As part of the local political elite, their nomination and election as deputies are pro forma—clearly secondary to established high party position and/or high state office in the local organs. As reported in Chapter III, the secretary of the people's council, the first vice-president and sometimes one vice-president (in larger councils) enter the local political elite through state channels, and have somewhat lower party positions than other vice-presidents and, of course, the council president who is the party chairman (first secretary). For all these individuals, no one decides whether or not they should become a deputy.

If a man is one of the local party secretaries of a municipality who fills a vice-presidency of the people's council, there is no "debate" as to whether or not he would make a "good" deputy—not by the party leadership and probably not by the citizens in the district allotted to him, for the residents are certainly astute enough to recognize the benefit of having a party secretary as deputy from their locale. If a new party secretary is to become a council vice-president, connoting a personnel change in the local political elite, the announcement that a party secretary is a deputy nominee indicates that he *will* be "elected" as a council vice-president at the first meeting after elections.

People's Councils 93

When a people's council first vice-president or secretary position must be filled (for whatever reason), the source of replacements is not the highest echelons of the local party, but mid-level party activists whose expertise (as a lawyer, economist, etc., in cities, or other specialties in rural areas) would be essential for governmental administration at that level and location. While the entrance of such individuals into the local political elite is certain to be a matter of discussion for the Party's bureau and among party secretaries, the following allocation of deputy posts to new members of the political elite is of minor significance, and arrangements can be made to introduce districts' citizens to their soon-to-be deputy on short notice (e.g., by sending him to speak before a citizen's committee or two). At the commune level, the proportion of non-professional party members (described above) in the executive committee increases for the simple reason that fewer full-time party workers are available for top people's council posts. In the smallest communes, one *may* find the permanent bureau itself to include one or two such individuals.

Even in the smallest people's council, however, the political elite are but a few deputies among many. A second and larger group of deputies is what I have roughly labeled as "the needed," i.e., functionaries needed by the state to administer and, by the Party, for advice in decision-making. Again, these people are in the councils primarily as a recognition of their positions in state organs or in their careers, since they (in most cases) hold no post of responsibility in the Party. These are the educated, the expert, and the loyal; managing and directing developmental/modernization efforts, their integration into local political institutions is essential. Partly co-opted by their very membership in the Party (seen by most as necessary for career and job security), "the needed" are advanced on the basis of their talents and subservience; they are not party activists, but party servants. Such promotions bring "the needed" nearer the political elite in posts where they head departments of the local state bureaucracy, administer schools, preside over courts, direct banking and finance, supervise health and sanitation, and so on.

Promotion to these types of posts virtually obliges an individual to become a deputy. A doctor, upon becoming a community's sole physician, becomes a deputy immediately. In these instances, as one county deputy in Iași told me, "it is assumed by everyone" that he was to be a deputy.[106] For a person "needed" by the political elite, this is usually accomplished through recommendation from a relevant group of

DEMOCRATIC CENTRALISM IN ROMANIA

professionals—architects, doctors, etc., to the S.U.F. which, in turn, proposes that individual to the voters of a certain district. Particularly in the case of deputies for districts in a county-level people's council, the proposed individual need not be a resident in the district he represents. For people in the "needed" category, whose specialty usually requires city dwelling, deputies are, at best, relatives of someone in the commune they represent; often there is no connection at all. In communes or smaller towns there is, of course, a much greater correlation between where a deputy resides and the district he represents.

Some of "the needed" become members of the people's council executive committee (but not the bureau). In that capacity, as well as in their day-to-day duties heading local enterprises, agencies, etc., these deputies provide the expertise (technical or social) that the political elite requires for rational decision-making and administration of centrally-decreed policies. There are other "needed" individuals, however, who might not hold top posts in the local economy, administration, or culture, but who have that potential. Party membership, of course, comes first for these individuals, but becoming a deputy usually follows shortly.

A final category of deputies constitutes "the fillers," needed by the local political elite as a group but not as individuals. Abstractly, they partly fulfill a requirement of governments everywhere—to legitimize rule through the representation of a broad popular base. Actually, this group of deputies is not representative of the "masses" of Romanians in significant respects. This is particularly true when considering the party membership and educational levels.

Typically, eighty to ninety percent of a municipality's deputies are party members,[107] while in rural communes the proportion of party members is usually around two-thirds of the council. In either case, deputies are not representative of a population in which only eleven percent are party members. Moreover, far more deputies have completed their education through secondary levels and/or university than the entire population. In the general population, the ratio of lyceum (high school) to elementary school (eighth grade) graduates is usually one to four or one to three;[108] among deputies, except in rural communes that ratio is often reversed.

When election time arrives, or when a vacancy exists between elections, deputies of this last category are proposed, nominated and then elected through mechanisms that are formally similar to what "needed" and elite

People's Councils

deputies go through as well, but in ways such that some interplay exists between popular sentiment and the Party's wishes—more so in some regions than in others. That locations vary as to how less important deputies are chosen can be inferred from the more specific answers to Question Twenty-two where differences were seen between Iași and Brașov counties. Iași deputies tended to think that their skills, expertise, etc., were most responsible for their selection whereas Brașov deputies answered most often that party or front organization activities brought about their nomination.

This *may* indicate that in Iași, expertise or skills impress citizens and party alike more than activism in the Party or related organizations. On the other hand, such responses might indicate(and this is a possibility of importance for the potential of a dialectic approach) that the political elite can less effectively procure deputy candidates who are active in the Party or its front organizations in a locality where it (the Party) has promoted modernization/development at a rapid pace from a lower socio-economic level.

We have, of course, seen indications before that such might be the case in Iași, and perhaps in less developed/modernized areas generally that are changing faster. Deputies seem to enter public life for different reasons in Iași (i.e., a public "need") and somewhat later than in Brașov (Question Nine), while having had less activity in the Party or front organizations prior to becoming deputies than Brașov counterparts (Question Eleven), but more current activity in non-political organizations (Question Fourteen). Information from Question Twenty-two, then, falls into place with other more quantifiable measures, suggesting that local politics in Romania, insofar as the selection of deputies is concerned, is diverse in ways corresponding to differences in the rapidity of modernization/development.

Aside from such considerations, it *is* true that a constant effort is exerted by the local political elite to assure the appearance of "representativeness" in the people's council at their level as to occupations, sex, and particularly nationalities. The local party bureau and people's council permanent bureau, together and separately (they often meet as one body), consider the council's membership and, from lower party activists, receive recommendations as to what individuals would be best to fill the less important council vacancies. The county-level political elite, for instance, is informed by town, city, and commune elites of deputy candidates to

96   DEMOCRATIC CENTRALISM IN ROMANIA

the county level. In communes, such a recommendation procedure often does not exist since the political elite has at its disposal fairly complete knowledge of potential deputies.

Meetings of mass "organizations of working people" are then held, pursuant to a 1966 Law of Elections,[109] where individuals are verbally proposed as potential candidates for deputy. In effect, an organization "endorses" someone at such meetings and, for any given constituency, different meetings may propose different candidates. In practice, this has almost never been done, although some deputies privately advocted change in that direction. Much more often, two and more organizations will propose the same person for a constituency—not surprising since party activities at all such meetings convey the Party's judegments regarding potential candidates.

Discussion at such meetings is allowed and does take place, but only in exceptional circumstances is serious objection made to proposed individuals. If not themselves present at such a meeting, less important condidates are subsequently told of their proposal, and are often genuinely surprised.[110] The citizens' proposal is then considered by the executive bureau of the S.U.F. and, finally, by the S.U.F. local council. Once nominated by the Socialist Unity Front (at least 30 days before the election), the candidate must officially accept the nomination in writing at the electoral commission for his constituency. Unless ill, physically or mentally, most rational Romanians accept the honor.

The electoral commission of the constituency then introduces the nominee to the public via posters, newspaper announcements or mass meetings. In the subsequent few days, it is legally possible for "any organization of the working people and any citizen of the Socialist Republic of Romania" to "lodge a complaint against the acceptance or rejection" of a candidate. While this *has* been done, necessitating new nominations, citizens almost always choose to forever hold their collective peace.

As a sidelight to all of this, one is led to ask why any politically less-than-active Romanian citizen would want to be a deputy. In discussions related to Question Twenty-two I gained insights into the attitude of deputies about their positions. First, there accrues to deputies a genuine increase in status. While most Romanians recognize, I think, the limiations under which a deputy assumes that post, most subjects interviewed said being a deputy gained them respect in their community.

People's Councils 97

A significant proportion of deputies emphasized the "moral" rewards from their job—that is, the sense of personal accomplishment. One might doubt that this sense of accomplishment, among deputies outside the political elite, could be derived from any influence on policy-making. Nevertheless, it was apparent that all deputies serve their constituency in some, though perhaps small, ways.

Relatively few deputies mentioned other reasons why they wanted to be elected. Yet the few who told of other enticements for being a people's council member indicated to me evidence for what I had already suspected. While deputies are not paid salaries (unless they are people's council officers), there are remunerations of sorts. First, housing is more easily received by deputies than other citizens. In Romania, as in most socialist countries, housing continues to be a large problem and waiting lists exist for apartment buildings that are only in the planning stages. Being a deputy often enables one to circumvent those lists, and obtain new apartments in more desireable locations. I found this practice more prevalent in some areas than in others. In Braşov County, to cite an example, the practice is sufficiently entrenched that an unmarried female deputy, without dependants, was able to procure a new apartment of five rooms. For many Romanians, five rooms would suffice for a family of four with grandparents.

In Cluj, deputies indicated that preferential treatment at food stores was common (better produce, quicker service, etc.). One Timiş deputy told of tax reductions possible for deputies since any awards and/or medals from the state, often given to deputies, reduce one's payments. Meanwhile it is possible for the children of deputies in Iaşi County, said a deputy there, to more easily gain university admission and find a better job upon graduation. Since so few of these responses were given, I cannot say how generalizable such "remunerations" are for deputies. That they exist at all, however, is some indication that being a deputy is not without its benefits.

Because most of the questionnaire's items measured opinions at one point in time, I meant Question Twenty-three as a means to gain a comparative index of change over time in people's councils. Responses, however, were relatively unproductive from the point of view of this study. The item asked if, given Romania's economic and social development in the past decade, the activities of the people's council had become more important and complex, had remained the same, or had simplified.

98 DEMOCRATIC CENTRALISM IN ROMANIA

Almost without exception, deputies answered with response "A"—more complex and important. Very small percentages were scored in either of the other categories. One can probably interpret such answers to mean that an almost universal opinion is shared among Romanian people's council deputies—that the councils *are* more important and more complex relative to a decade earlier. It does not follow, of course, that people's councils are *much* more important in the mid-1970s than the early to mid-1960s. Yet, if the deputies thought that councils had no powers at all a decade ago, and have only a few more responsibilities today, then their answers were honestly given.

Deputies were asked, in the questionnaire's twenty-fourth item, to name new "attributes" (i.e., legal powers or areas of competence) of their people's council. Iași County was found to have the highest percentages in categories labeled "more activity," "new functions," and "other." (See Table XVIII.) At the same time, Brașov County led in the "does not know" classification, while the largest proportion of deputies answering "greater autonomy and/or independence" occurred in Timiș County.

These scores suggest what changes made the strongest impact on deputies in each county. The percentages do not indicate, of course, precisely what changes *did* occur over time. Many local political leaders assert that any changes instituted in Romanian local government have been uniform intrs-nationally.[111] That may well be so, from the perspective of those deciding to make structural or functional alterations. Nevertheless, if people's councils were not alike prior to changes, it seems probable that any nation-wide alterations could not be applied evenly relative to each locality, thus leading to different deputy observations.

The uniformly large scores in the "do not know" category are, of themselves, interesting. That such large proportions of all counties' deputies, and particularly Brașov's council members, had no solid impressions of recent changes can mean only one of three things—that there were so many "new attributes" that no one stands out, that they did not want to comment on the question, or that no significant "new attributes" had been given to their people's councils. The degree to which each of these possibilities explains high "do not know" scores probably varies from one county to another as much as the scores themselves.

Iași County's lead in the classifications "more activity," and "new functions" may be important for this study. Well over one-third of Iași's

TABLE XVIII

Question Twenty-four: New Attributes of People's Councils in Opinion of Deputies

Category of Answer	N = 37 Timiş % (weighted)	N = 47 Cluj % (weighted)	N = 50 Braşov % (weighted)	N = 64 Iaşi % (weighted)
Greater Autonomy and Independence	44.1	36.8	23.8	5.4
More Activity	11.8	17.5	13.3	22.7
New Functions	8.6	4.5	10.5	13.4
Don't Know	18.7	23.1	39.9	28.6
Other	16.7	18.1	12.5	29.8
Totals	99.9%	100.0%	100.0%	99.9%

N = 198
(.01 = P > .001)

100 DEMOCRATIC CENTRALISM IN ROMANIA

deputies (weighted sample) gave one of these two answers. This tends to suggest that in the least "advanced" but most rapidly changing county in socio-economic terms, deputies saw their councils doing *more* of what they had previously done as well as performing additional and new tasks —both to a greater extent than in other counties where change is at a slower pace from relatively higher socio-economic levels.

Meanwhile, Iaşi's distinctly low score in the "greater autonomy/independence" category does not necessarily point to less of those qualities in that county. Instead, one can suggest that *relative* to the past situation (in whatever past time was the deputies' reference point), Iaşi deputies might not have noticed a significant change in the direction of greater autonomy or independence. If their councils operated with a fair degree of independence before, then one can understand their reference to other "new attributes" as being relatively more important now.

Finally, the Iaşi scores can be seen to be considerably more diverse. Within the classification labeled "other," Iaşi deputies gave a wide range of answers, none of which exceeded the proportions scored by the principal answers listed (although "more expertise and specialization" did score approximately 5.0% in Iaşi).

Comparing Iaşi and Braşov counties does not, obviously, suggest dichotomous results from Question Twenty-four. There does not appear to be a direct relationship between this measure and either a socio-economic level or a rate of modernization/development. Again, however, one finds a strong indication that Iaşi's more rapidly changing environment from a less advanced stage of development is coincident with an expanding political life (where deputies are more impressed than in other counites by the increasing activtiy and new functions of their people's council, and where deputies evince the greatest diversity of opinion). Because this questionnaire item did not find contrasting results in Braşov County, however, it is more difficult to relate these results directly to a dialectical hypothesis. At this point, then, one cannot be assured that any county's scores are related to that region's rate of change or socio-economic level.

An index was sought of deputies' assessments of people's council debate through Question Twenty-five. This can, in turn, be compared with earlier-obtained measures of problems facing the people's councils. Thus, item Twenty-five asked what the subject of most debate was in each deputy's council. A short list of topics was provided verbally,

People's Councils 101

concluding with the opportunity for "other" responses. As with Question Sixteen data, deputies were allowed to give as many responses as they wished. Such a procedure enabled me to find a mean number of "debated topics" mentioned by deputies from each county, and also did not confine responses to categories provided in the questionnaire.

Deputies from all counties tended to rank industry, public maintenance and services, provisioning, education, and agriculture as principal topics of debate. The order in which these topics took precedence varied, of course. For example, Iaşi deputies from rural localities overwhelmingly headed their list with agriculture and Iaşi deputies generally were somewhat more conscious of debate on education-related problems than deputies in other counties.

For the most part, therefore, replies to Question Twenty-five reconfirmed a previously-cited conclusion—that people's council deputies and their councils are locally-minded, focusing attention on problems of regional or parochial concern *more* than Five-Year Plans and the like. Even insofar as deputies said their councils debated about "industry," discussion centered not around how to increase production, but how to make factories more compatible with their surroundings, how to improve the lot of workers, etc. This leads to (understandably so) a differentiation among people's councils as to the topics discussed and foci of their concern.

As indicated above, however, this question *did* provide a quantitative measure that might be more directly relevant to considering a dialectic approach—namely an "average" number of "topics debated" mentioned by deputies at the location and level indicated below:

Level	Location			
	Timiş	Cluj	Braşov	Iaşi
Town-City	2.70	2.41	2.50	3.10
County	2.33	2.67	2.25	2.90
Commune	2.27	1.56	1.90	2.32

The score for "Town-City" in Timiş County means, for example, that the 23 deputies in that level mentioned 62 topics of debate in their councils, or a mean of 2.70.

Weighting such responses by location, as with Question Sixteen, produced the distribution below:

Level	Location			
	Timiş	Cluj	Braşov	Iaşi
Town-City	12.96	16.18	28.60	14.88
County	3.80	5.64	7.43	7.77
Commune	69.50	59.53	66.97	131.08
Total	86.26	81.35	103.00	153.73
Mean Responses Per Deputy (weighted)	2.33	1.73	2.06	2.40

Because there were no extreme cases in any of the counties to cause a distortion of the mean (if one or two deputies had mentioned an abnormally large number of "topics debated"), such a measure of central tendency probably gives us a good comparative index of the level of debate in people's councils in these counties (as the deputies perceive that debate). One must, of course, remember that the term "debate," as used here and in the questonnaire, need not connote the sense of advocates for two or more viewpoints openly arguing their positions in a public forum. Instead, one should assume that the deputies regard "debate" to include what an observer might label "discussion," "reports," or "points of information."

Readily apparent from the above scores is Iaşi County's consistent lead in the mean number of "topics debated" mentioned by deputies. Prior to such information (and prior to data from Question Sixteen), one might have expected in the more complex and diversified life of Braşov County that (1) more problems would exist and (2) people's councils would, thus, discuss a wider range of topics than councils in Iaşi. To the degree that we can rely on deputies' impressions, however, there is no evidence to lend credence to such ostensibly plausible assumptions. In fact, deputies tend to give opposite impressions—i.e., that Iaşi County leads in both categories.

We have, then, two indications (Questions Sixteen and Twenty-five) that Iaşi's people's councils are generally confronted by more problems and, correspondingly, discuss a wider vareity of topics. More important for this study, however, is the tentative relationship that seems to exist between a county's rate of socio-economic change and the scores resulting from Questions Sixteen and Twenty-five. If people's councils' discussion covers a wider range of problems in places that are changing most quickly,

People's Councils 103

then it may be that the Party's own efforts at rapid socio-economic change correlate with such political occurrences. In other words, an aspect of the dialectics of development may be apparent.

Like the questionnaire's twenty-first item, Question Twenty-six sought an indication of citizen-local government interaction. This time, however, the focus was on citizens' communications to deputies and local political institutions rather than means of political communication used by sub-national government to inform and/or mobilize the citizens. Asked "What type of problems do citizens raise?", deputies were given five choices:

A) proposals of a general or public character;
B) proposals of a personal character;
C) claims and complaints of a general or public character;
D) claims and complaints of a personal character;
E) others—which?

Answers in categories "B" and "D" might best be seen as representative of the "parochial" element in these counties' political communication, while "A" and "C" are indicative of greater public or community identi-fication. One cannot be sure, of course, that deputies' opinions regarding the nature of citizens' problems or needs necessarily reflect the political culture of that area; that is, after all, an indirect kind of measurement. It seems fair to say, however, that conventional wisdom would relate less "advanced" locales with more parochial viewpoints.[112] Data gained from Question Twenty-six, however, do not support such an assumption as strongly as might have been expected.

Instead (see Table XIX), total percentages in category "A" are higher in Iaşi than in Cluj County and near the Timiş score. Furthermore, the highest "B" score (a parochialism indicator) was in Cluj, second in Timiş, and Iaşi, third. Thus, while Iaşi County *does* have a lower percentage of responses in category "A" than Braşov (and higher in "B") as one would expect, the suspicion arises that some intervening variable is present causing citizens in a less developed/modernized area to be more public-minded than expected.

Also important for our purposes are cumulative scores for the C, D, and E categories which indicated together a measure of complaints and, possibly conflict between citizens and local government. Relative to A and

TABLE XIX
Question Twenty-six: Nature of Problems Raised by Citizens

Category	N = 37 Timiş % (weighted)	N = 47 Cluj % (weighted)	N = 50 Braşov % (weighted)	N = 64 Iaşi % (weighted)
A	33.4	29.7	46.8	32.5
B	57.4	63.3	44.2	54.6
C	4.6	1.4	9.0	7.6
D	4.6	5.1	—	5.4
E	—	.4	—	—
Totals	100.0%	99.9%	100.0%	100.1%

N = 198 (P > .10)

People's Councils   105

B classifications, few deputies gave these alternative responses. Nevertheless, it may be significant that Iași County led in this regard with approximately 13%, Timiș second with about 9.2%, and Brașov ahead of Cluj.

These measures tend to suggest that citizens in less socio-economically
"advanced" areas, where modernization/development is occurring more
quickly, have some cause to be *more* community-minded than citizens
in areas not changing as quickly—even though, like Timiș and Cluj, the
latter may be relatively more advanced. Moreover, citizens in fast-changing
places may be more vocal in their complaints—more ready to challenge
governmental institutions at a local level. Because these data are not
significant, one's conclusions must be guarded. If true, however, such
inferences from Question Twenty-six data support a dialectical hypothesis,
insofar as a regime which fosters socio-economic change reaps results
antithetical to its own direction of political life in return for its socio-
economic policies.

E: Summary

The backgrounds and opinions of people's council deputies presented
in this chapter imply several generalizable conclusions.

First, the *diversity* of local political life in a communist party state
such as Romania was revealed many times in the deputies' responses
(county to county differences were statistically significant in most tables).
Counties were found to be dissimilar with respect to deputies backgrounds,
in terms of when and how deputies entered politics as well as in terms
of their motivations for initial participation. The county to county differences seen in Questions Nine, Ten, and Eleven are clearly related
(Kendall's W, a multiple correlation statistic for ordinal data, = .91).
Early politicization and prior party involvement are most strongly rooted
in Brașov County, least so in Iași County. Socio-economic *levels* appear
to be directly related to such important political distinctions between
areas in Romania.

Question Fourteen, however, gave the first indication that levels of
modernization/development alone do not help explain other aspects of
political diversity. Iași deputies, who are more active outside the Party
than deputies in the other researched counties, also gave responses to
succeeding questions that implied support for a dialectical approach.

106 DEMOCRATIC CENTRALISM IN ROMANIA

Question Sixteen and, later, Question Twenty-five found Iaşi deputies consistently to mention more problems facing the people's council and more topics debated by the council than did deputies in other counties. Data from both of these items also lent further support to the portrayal of sub-national politics in Romania as exceedingly diverse.

Other questions gained details on aspects of local politics such as interest-groups, citizen-government interaction and deputy dissatisfaction. In the latter case, Question Eighteen found Iaşi deputies more willing to voice their dissatisfaction with certain aspects of their people's council (i.e., Iaşi had smaller percentages of deputies who said that no improvements were needed) than deputies elsewhere. Moreover, the kinds of suggestions made were less often innocuous and more often bearing directly on the nature of Romania's sub-national political system.

Question Twenty, data from which pointed to greater activity by "non-political organizations" attempting to influence public life in Iaşi County, gave credence to the suspicion that political life was less moribund in that part of Romania (where modernization/development is most rapid) than in other of the researched counties. The twenty-first item implied, as well, that the party and structures such as citizens' committees were less common means of interesting citizens in public life than were personal contacts by deputies and educational efforts where the pace of socio-economic change was highest. Moreover, Question Twenty-six found Iaşi citizens to be more prone to raise complaints and somewhat less parochial in the problems they were bringing to deputies than in counties less rapidly changing.

Taken together, data from the deputy questionnaire provide strong indications that political life in Romania is not uniform, and that it varies in ways that tend to form patterns (e.g., so that one can say politicization apparently occurs earlier in Braşov County among the four researched locales). But there is also sufficient indication that political diversity in Romania is influenced by socio-economic changes called modernization/development—and vice-versa. Particularly important are the opinions of people's council deputies as to activities outside the party, dissatisfaction with people's councils, influence by non-political organizations in local public life, and citizen public-mindedness combined with a willingness to complain. In each of these respects, Iaşi leads among the counties considered.

People's Councils   107

There exists sufficient cause, then, on the basis of answers given by deputies from sub-national levels, to suggest that a communist party regime which accelerates modernization/development to a rapid pace may, by doing so, foster political phenomena antithetical to its self-perceived interests.

This does not mean, of course, that deputies' opinions give one any reason to believe Romania's more rapidly changing areas are now or will become threats to Ceauşescu or his successors. The indications we have thus far of local political life in Romania provide no measure of the national regime's stability, its strengths or weaknesses. Moreover, not all the responses from deputies told of antithetical results that become more prominent where socio-economic change is fastest, and not all county to county differences were statistically significant. It may well be that Iaşi County and places like it in Romania are not changing as rapidly as they would have to in order to produce truly "disruptive" political consequences.

Thus, one ought to make no more profound conclusions at this point than what has been noted above: a communist party regime which promotes rapid socio-economic change is likely to incur, unintentionally, antithetical political results.

CHAPTER V

LOCAL POLITICAL ELITES

Were a dialectical hypothesis to explain politics in developing/modernizing states, then conflict and competition among sub-national political leaders over public policies are likely to exist, and vary from locale to locale according to their socio-economic level or rate of change.

Studies of communist party states are not lacking in an elite emphasis.[113] Moreover, seeing conflict between and among national-level elites is commonplace, particularly with regard to the Soviet leadership.[114] Since the mid-1960s, studies of communist elites have suggested that an increasingly technocratic criterion for elite recruitment exists in communist states, corresponding to a decline in ideology and the emergence of a managerial class.[115] Motivated by these expectations, demographic indices (e.g., career patterns and education) are used to explain the political behavior of leaders. The net effect of both old and new approaches to communist leadership has been to portray these elites, on the one hand, as in conflict and intrigue over who rules, while on the other hand to suggest incremental change in the nature of that conflict, as issues become less ideological and more technocratic. In other words, communist elites are still seen to be at each other's throats, but nowadays for different reasons.

Because political life in capital cities may not reflect accurately the manner in which communist leaders behave, however, this chapter is focused on local-level political elites in Romania as they are found in State and Party organs, comparing leaders from four counties regarding their policy goals and role perceptions. Two phenomena will be of particular interest, if present: (1) diversity *among* the counties and (2) the degree of conflict *within* each county relative to each other. It is important to emphasize the distinction between these two points. While recognizing that political ideas are not uniform in a communist party state is probably a necessary precondition for an intra-national test of a dialectical

108

Local Political Elites 109

hypothesis, one must take an additional step—to find out whether or not the extent of political conflict varies with socio-economic levels, or rates of socio-economic change.

"Conflict," of course, denotes something different here than common usage suggests; given the lack of access to meetings from the Party, I am only able to *infer* from comments made to me during interviews and group discussions that leaders conflict and/or compete with one another. Likewise, in observational settings, the role my presence played in altering behavior in small meetings of local political elites made the measurement of "conflict" suspect. Those circumstances required taking notice of subtle differences of opinion, and attempts to minimize dissenting roles.

Thus, when we speak of conflict and competition among sub-national political elites we look to the people in the highest organs of local government (the people's council permanent bureau which overlaps, almost entirely, with the party bureau for the same level), searching for differences of opinion over goals and role perceptions, i.e., what should be the principal concerns of local authorities, and how should sub-national leaders behave. In that context, one needs to know, quite simply, both the extent and nature of intra-elite conflict in each county relative to other counties.

B: BACKGROUNDS OF LOCAL POLITICAL ELITES

Personal interviews were conducted with forty-two individuals who occupy positions in permanent bureaus at various levels of sub-national Romanian govenment. In other cases, I held discussions with all or part of permanent bureaus my observation of a people's council, executive committee or permanent bureau session. These group discussions served to augment personal interviews.

Through neither of these means did I obtain a "scientific" sample. My informants were those political elites for whom being interviewed constituted no threat or interruption or both. Nevertheless, I was satisfied that my effort to interview *some* members of permanent bureaus from all levels in all subject counties had been generally successful (see Table XX). Moreover, the depth of each interview was a safeguard for their accuracy, almost always allowing cross-chelcks during the discussion to gauge the respondent's forthrightness.

TABLE XX

Distribution of Elite Interviews by County and Level

	Timiş	Cluj	Braşov	Iaşi	Totals
County	1	–	2	3	6
Town-City	5	3	2	4	14
Commune	2	6	5	9	22
Totals	8	9	9	16	42

In all instances, questions relating to the backgrounds of political elites were utilized. I was interested in the degree of intra-national diversity with respect to the type of people who become leaders in local political life. Following earlier studies of communist elites,[116] the information sought included:

—ages
—ethnic heritage
—education
—length of party membership
—social origins
—party education
—non-party organization membership
—sex
—past careers
   —party
   —military
   —education
   —technical
   —other

Rather quickly is was apparent that becoming a political elite-member in Romania implies fitting into a general "formula" for such background attributes. Unlike people's council deputies, who in many ways mirror the population's characteristics, but who have little impact on policy-making other than legitimization and communication functions, permanent

Local Political Elites

bureau members at *all* local levels seem to possess backgrounds that reflect implicit prerequisites in terms of social and political characteristics. I am not aware of any written standards for such individuals, but there can be little question as to the de facto selection process that involves (what I termed above) a "formula."

The pattern to which I am referring is produced by what, in the Soviet case, is known as the nomenklatura system. This system of "selection, assignment and dismissal"[117] for important cultural, economic, and especially political posts, while likely declining in the former two spheres, remains evident among political elites—evident in ways that will be discussed shortly.

"Nomenklatura" does not adequately describe the selection of local political elites, except to point out that in communist party states one sees a hierarchically-determined replenishment of leadership. Whether "recruited" from other party or state units or "co-opted" from other specialized careers, sub-national leaders are not solely the choice of other important political figures at that level. Instead, central party organs in Bucharest oversee the rise of people to the top in all counties, checking the records of nominees for vital party-state positions, potentially vetoing unacceptable names, and "urging" the selection of other individuals. Similarly, county officials watch the procedures of city, town, and commune levels.

While the specifics of how all this operates are cloudy, one can surmise that the commonsense self-interest of local party officials dictates compliance with the criteria for elite status established by central party organs. Local state organs, of course, apply the same standards. Since all leadership positions in the Party must (by party statute) be approved by the hierarchically superior party committee (in fact, the bureau), this constitutes a virtual power of appointment. Given that any people's council's permanent bureau is composed of the party leadership for that locale (i.e., party secretaries), that permanent bureau's composition is essentially determined by the same hierarchically superior party committee.

Of the permanent bureau members who are *not* local party leaders—the first vice-president and the secretary of the executive committee—the latter is appointed to that position "on the approval of the hierarchically superior state administration body of the executive committee."[118] Only the first vice-president is, then, a *local* political elite in the sense of being selected through processes relatively independent of higher organs. Nevertheless, he too is always, "responsible to" the "hierarchically superior executive committee" and Bucharest.[119]

DEMOCRATIC CENTRALISM IN ROMANIA

None of the foregoing comments, however, explains *why* the vestiges of a nomenklatura system survive. Earlier studies of communist political elites have pointed to a decline in ideology, the emergence of a managerial class, etc., corresponding to socio-economic changes. Communist regimes have an alternative, however, that enables the political elite to remain closed. As long as the Romanian Communist Party has allowed sufficient, albeit incremental changes in the composition of local leadership, it has maintained a hold on political appointments. In the broadest sense, those adroit and/or necessary "changes" meant altering the criteria for entering the political elite to fit socio-economic changes.

An official policy to that effect was clearly established by Ceauşescu as early as 1972 by which the replenishment of political elites would be accomplished on the basis of revised criteria:

> . . . over the years some erroneous views had been advanced to the effect that it were enough to have some experience of life or, as we used to say in the past, to have a good social origin, for being able to solve any problem. Undoubtedly, experience of life, revolutionary past and social origin are important. . . they, however, are not enough so as to enable our cadres to adequately run various sections of society's activities. To carry out in a satisfactory way the great tasks that confront our Party, a thorough scientific, political and professional training as well as a high level of organizational and managerial skill is required of every cadre; we should also consider these as basic criteria to be met by Party and State activists. . . . [120]

The selection of local leadership remains, therefore, a closed process, but with the criteria for recruitment changed. Therefore, backgrounds of the sub-national political elite reflect, almost in unison, a shift—an imposed similarity, so to speak.

Ages, for example, of local political elites were remarkably uniform when this research was conducted. Of individuals interviewed, no one was older than fifty-two years or younger than thirty years. More indicative of a central tendency, however, was that about two-thirds of the elites were 38 through 45 years of age (27 people). Thus, the leadership cohort that participated as mature adults in the early communist regime of the late 1940s and early 1950s no longer dominates local elite positions.

Local Political Elites 113

Such an age homogenity means that, when those leaders had been selected (1968-69), a concerted effort had been made by central party officials to effect a transition between cohorts. At the sub-national levels, there was significant evidence of such a transition as, within the sample, only a few individuals had held positions of equal responsibility prior to 1968. This was particularly apparent in Iaşi where first vice-president Tiron, secretary Andrei, and vice-president Ştefanescu had all taken their posts since 1969.

Other background characteristics show similar changes. As Ceauşescu implied in the quotation cited above, the original criterion of a "correct" social class, i.e., worker or peasant background, is being set aside. For over twenty years, there was no doubt that such an origin was a prerequisite for achieving a post of high responsibility, even at the local level. There had been, in Romania, a period when workers became lawyers, judges, mayors, etc., literally overnight, and when instant academic degrees had been conferred on party leaders.[121] Some of the current political elite, who had been youthful observers of events after World War II, now reflect with disgust on such events. One man in a high party-state position said caustically that "Romania, it seems, adopted a strange form of communism; egalitarian only in the sense of leveling off at the lowest level."[122]

Another official, however, argued that in recent years, following Ceauşescu's lead, the situation has been rectified—that in Romanian politics, "like muddy water, it has taken some time for the dirt to settle."[123] By the late 1960s and particularly in the early 1970s, incapable party leaders have, indeed, been replaced by specialists in administration, law, engineering, and economics. It was often the case that such specialists were not children of workers, foremen, or technicians. There is, for example, no uniformity regarding the social origins of interviewed elites such that one could infer a continued preference for the "correct" background; people from "middle-class" or "bourgeois" background are now present at all levels of sub-national elites. One must, therefore, distinguish between PCR propaganda that cites statistics for party *committees* showing forty-five to fifty percent of those committee members as "working class" *vis-a-vis* the reality of political power at the local level. The Party bureaus and secretariats (where decisions are made) do not reflect committee's overall membership.

More revealing of the extent to which the replenishment of local elites is now based on different criteria is the education and training of

such individuals. A fairly typical line-up of personnel for a large city's permanent bureau, is in the city of Cluj (population over 200,000) which boasted an economist, a mathematics professor, two mechanical engineers, a construction engineer, and a lawyer.[124] That a permanent bureau, and therefore the corresponding party elite as well, includes such highly educated professionals is not to suggest a domination of sub-national elites by co-opted individuals. To the contrary, obtaining a university degree is now *expected* for an ambitious party activist.

The day of the Party "ideologue," sans expertise is a substantive field, appears to be waning in local Romanian politics. The most advantageous route for political advancement appears to be party activism *plus* a judicious combination of higher education and political "savvy." Although educated and expert individuals "needed" by the elite *are* co-opted from established careers into the Party and local government—usually no further than the people's council executive committee—this mechanism, while it "siphons-off" socio-economic interests and assists political elites in policy formulation and implementation, is not part of the change in elite recruitment criteria to which I have referred. Instead, there seem to be two distinct, but related, developments—Party leadership requiring expert advice and then being told that it, too, must gain the specialization needed in a modernizing/developing system:

> ...the entire Party and State apparatus must realize that the solution of the great problems of socialist construction requires a high level of training and competence....I refer first of all to the acquisition of a thorough knowledge in the ideological, organizational, and managerial fields so as to enable the cadres to adequately understand and solve the increasingly complex problems of socio-economic socialist construction in our country.[125]

For the two permanent bureau members not in the local party secretariat or bureau, the first vice-president and the executive committee secretary, the demand for expertise has become universal. For the country and municipality levels, all first vice-presidents with whom I spoke had degrees in engineering, economics, law, and occasionally other fields such as mathematics. Communal people's councils required no such expertise, of course, but many of the first vice-presidents at that level

Local Political Elites   115

had technical training beyond the lyceum (high school), often in agronomy, and a few did have university degrees. Secretaries of cities' or counties' people's councils usually had post-graduate degees in law, which has become mandatory since a 1971 statute.[126] In towns, and certainly in communes, other education or training suffices (military officer, accountant, etc.) given that the individual has attended additional training for council secretaries that is offered by the administrative department of the county-level people's council.

With very few exceptions, I found a high degree of relevant training for people in leadership positions, no doubt a direct reflection of the strong emphasis given to improving the competence of all cadre, repeatedly stated in texts and internal propaganda messages.[127]

Thus far, one can see the effects of changed criteria for entering (or staying in) the sub-national political elite. Nevertheless, other criteria for political elites status have not changed. For example, of elites interviewed, only two were female. One might expect that a communist regime's rhetorical commitment to sexual equality should be reflected in local leadership. In fact, the Romanian leadership is no less male-dominated than other European political systems and, in terms of the highest posts in local political life, perhaps more so. Women *are* regularly included in people's council executive committees and in party committees; among party secretaries and permanent bureau members, however, women are very much under-represented (even as compared with their one-fourth to thirty percent presence in people's councils). Simply put, decisions about public policy are made exclusively by males in Romania.

Ethnic heritage has also remained a stable criterion for elite status. Succinctly stated, being Romanian as opposed to German, Hungarian, Jewish, etc., is preferable in terms of political advancement. There are, to be sure, some of each of these minorities in the higher echelons of local government where large communities of those groups reside. But only in the counties where one "minority" is, in fact, a majority (for example, Magyars in Mureş county) does that group have more than symbolic (i.e., one person) representation in the local political elite. Usually, the people's council executive committee or party committee will include a small number of each minority. The political elite (the

116   DEMOCRATIC CENTRALISM IN ROMANIA

people's council permanent bureau, party bureau, and secretariat) invariably is composed of people of the Romanian nationality.

One must carefully distinguish between minority presence in the
political elite as opposed to general membership in the Party or people's
councils. Romanian publications boldly announce that minorities are
"faithfully reflecting" in the composition of "all state bodies." Moreover, the Party unites the population "irrespective of nationality."[128]
Taken at face value, these assertions are accurate. As noted previously,
however, the leadership is insulated from "faithfully reflected" population composition. Timiş, Cluj and Braşov, for example, despite large
minority populations were not "representative" of the population's ethnic
composition in permanent bureaus in major cities or at the county level.

Specific requirements relating to a person's party background have
likewise been modified little, if at all. To become one of the political
elite at any sub-national level still involves, necessarily, lengthy prior
activity in the Communist Party. But several changes with respect to this
criterion are, nonetheless, important.

1) While extensive party involvement remains necessary, no quantity
of time or effort on the Party's behalf is, today, "sufficient" to
elevate an individual into the local political elite.

2) The "length" of prior party involvement necessary is not fixed;
depending upon what other qualities a potential local leader had
to offer, this criterion may be reduced or increased.

3) The kind of activity necessarily implies more than nominal membership in the Party; local political elites, with very few exceptions,
exhibit records of leadership in party cells, in the U.T.C., or in
the military party organizations. Proven ability to assume responsibility is a more important criterion as time goes on.

The first two of the above points are, of course, related. Years of party
membership or servile obedience are not (in the 1970s) qualities that can
alone assure either advancement to, or maintenance of, political elite
status. Instead, several deputies interviewed had been "demoted" from

Local Political Elites

leadership positions while still in their 50s despite many years of dedicated party work. On the other hand, of all elites interviewed, about half had fewer than fifteen years of regular party membership.

The four counties were not significantly different in terms of average years of prior party membership of interviewed elites (from about 14-16 years). While this is a gross estimate, of course, it may be indicative of the general magnitude of party experience that is "necessary" (if not sufficient) for sub-national elite status. If fifteen years is often the length of party service needed for elite status, there are many exceptions. When exceptions are made reveals a good deal about the directions now being taken in elite recruitment. In Iaşi county, where the length of party experience for leaders averaged slightly less than in other countries, I found a tendency to advance quickly those individuals with relevant expertise. A thirty-six-year-old city first vice-president, for example, with a law degree at the age of 22 in 1959, and a party member from his student days, became a deputy in 1964, council secretary in 1965, a vice-president in 1969 and first vice-president in 1971. In the same city, a man of 39 who jointed the U.T.C. as a law student in the early 1960s, and the regular party a few years later, was elevated to the council secretary position in 1969 from his position as legal consultant for the people's council (a bureaucratic department of the council). There is no question that other men, with greater party seniority, were by-passed to promote these youthful, but skilled individuals.

Political elite status is, then, dependent on the competency a person can bring to a position of responsibility as well as necessary commitments to the Party measured in both years of service and extent of activity. There can be, and often is, an implicit "trade-off" for certain cases, where the necessary length and kind of an individual's party experience is reduced in light of higher education, pertinent expertise, etc. Such a compromise has been institutionalized in the case of first vice-presidents and council secretaries whose relatively high competence (usually in law) is routinely accepted in lieu of high party standing.

The "kind" of activity to which I made reference above is that of a *cadre*, i.e., a communist in a social, economic or political role that involves personal responsibility for command-type decisions. Cadres are the Party's functionaries or workers, overseeing the implementation of party policies. Before entering the local political elite, any individual

118   DEMOCRATIC CENTRALISM IN ROMANIA

must exhibit his or her worth to the Party in low-level cadre positions, down to the "prosaic tasks of factory administration, the repair of houses and the running of public bath-houses."[129] There are, subsequently, more glamorous positions for cadres—as a director of a financial institution, an editor of a major publication, a military commander, or chairman of an academic faculty, etc. The key point is that a party membership card is never a ticket to elite status. In the context of party goals and needs, an individual's "mettle" must be tested in such a post.

Interviews revealed *no* exceptions to this rule. Even in the smallest commune, the people's council president (party chairman for the commune) and other members of the permanent bureau had all either held communal posts of responsibility previously, or were continuing to do so at that time. At the commune level, cadre positions were often that of president of a cooperative farm, foreman of a lumbering operation, chief of police and school director. This demand for cadre experience has equalized and surpassed the factor of political reliability as a *necessary* component in assessing an individual's party background.

"Cadre experience," as a component of the party background criterion for elite status has, however, also changed. The *positions* an individual might have held in the past to provide command-type experience are, alone, no denotation of today's cadre in the PCR. Party education is now perhaps the definitive way to identify a cadre who has a chance of becoming a political elite. Political elites at the local level must be experienced cadre in the sense of having held posts of responsibility, but must *also* be politically educated, i.e., have been subjected to indoctrination at the Party's schools and institutes in Bucharest.

Ceauşescu has insisted on the need for strengthening the political education of cadre upon many occasions. Evident in the General Secretary's pronouncements is the concern that socio-economic changes (development/modernization) may lessen the Party's ideological reins on its own membership:

> . . . we have a series of results in the educational and ideological activity . . . which demonstrate that our Party, the comrades active in these domains have concerned themselves with equipping the Party members politically and ideologically, with ensuring the higher socialist consciousness of our entire people. *But these results are*

Local Political Elites   119

*not up to current demands and especially do not tally with achieve-
ments in other domains of activity.*[130] (Emphasis added).

The connection of party education to leadership has also been made
explicit by Ceauşescu, establishing clear distinctions among mere party
membership, technical specialization and party training:

> . . .it is necessary to raise the political and ideological level of
> the Party and State active, of the leading cadres, of all the Party
> members. To be a Party and State leader, to be a Party and State
> activist presupposes a good Marxist-Leninist ideological training.
> Without this, nobody will be able to creditably fulfill the tasks
> entrusted by the Party. I am stressing this because it seems that
> a certain concept has appeared, namely that if one has some
> technical and professional knowledge and if one concerns one-
> self with the resolving of such issues it suffices for being a leader.
> No, comrades, this alone does not suffice! No matter how fine
> a specialist somebody might be, and we need specialists and
> must insist on improving specialist knowledge, he who fails to
> concern himself with raising his ideological and political level
> cannot be a Party and State leader. He may be an efficient
> specialist, a good office worker, but no political leader.[131]

Such a message is not atypical. Ceauşescu continues to evince a
wariness about the state of mind of the Party in light of socio-economic
changes the Party began slightly over a decade before. Admonitions
about ideological lapses go hand-in-hand with calls for greater competence and specialization.[132] It is at least incongruous for Ceauşescu
to strive for changes in the Party cadre that he, at the same time, fears
will damage the leadership's ideological hold on the membership;
perhaps one can see such a dilemma as one aspect of the dialectic
discussed at the outset of this study.

Thus, the criterion for sub-national political elites relating to party
background has been changed in several respects; the components
of that change were:

1)   the length of prior membership required no longer an absolute
     indicator for elite recruitment; now relative to other standards;

120 DEMOCRATIC CENTRALISM IN ROMANIA

2) an end to political reliability as a sufficient party background; now seen as co-extensive with standards below;

3) an increased importance attached to competence in a specialized field (technical, legal, etc.);

4) an increased importance given to demonstrating one's combination of competence and political loyalty as a cadre in a post of responsibility; the *kind* of party activity, therefore, is a more important consideration;

5) an increased demand for subsequent party education (indoctrination) *beyond* both specialized expertise and performing in a post of responsibility.

These changes in party background requirements were effected over a period of at least two years (1970 and 1971). Prior to these changes, early in the 1960s, development/modernization had been accelerated. Late in the 1960s the demand for specialization and training, coordinated with the territorial-administrative reorganization of 1968, allowed a transition of leadership that continued into 1970. In 1970, the Party's political education program was completely reorganized, and in 1971 (after a Central Committee plenary session) Ceauşescu began to strongly re-emphasize political indoctrination. In the following three to four years, the Party leadership has continued to try to control what it had begun a decade earlier.

In practice, the recruiting activities of the Party now reflect changed criteria for its leadership. While no party rule states so, it is evident that three categories of members are sought. First, and most generally, people are sought who are "useful and valuable" but no more;[133] as tools of the leadership, these people will carry messages to the populace, and play a legitimizing role as "fillers" in people's councils and other social organizations. There are, however, two other ranks of party recruits—both more than "useful and valuable" (as any party member should be); they are, in fact, *needed*.

But people who are "needed" by the Party are two quite distinct types. There are, first, co-opted individuals who contribute to the specialized

Local Political Elites   121

organs of party and state, who have had equal or more education than the other "needed" recruits, but who have no policy-making role. They are experts, but not decision-makers in posts of responsibility; they are party members (often belatedly), but not activists.

On the other hand, there are "needed" individuals sought for their potential as political elite, particulary young persons "qualified in administration, economics, and technology"[134] who appear to combine such qualifications with a desire to be active in the Party (usually exhibited in the U.T.C.). If they qualify on those grounds, then these "needed" individuals must prove themselves, and they are channeled into cadre posts in social organizations, the military, economic enterprises, or the state administration. Grooming a person for a leadership role does not stop there, however, since one's credentials as a cadre are not complete until going to Bucharest for political "learning."

The principal "school" of the Party is the Ştefan Gheorghiu Academy for Social-Political Education, an academy within which are a wide assortment of institutes, generally divided into two main "departments." The many institutes (sometimes called faculties, centers, etc.) are scattered around Bucharest, often located in the mansions of a long-departed (but since replaced) aristocracy. Each institute specializes in the indoctrination of cadres assigned to a particular kind of function (e.g., journalists go to the Journalism Faculty). The first department is, overall, higher ranking, focusing on cadres in the Party itself and in mass organizations. The second indoctrinates state functionaries, economic managers and the like.

Many party members desire to attend these courses which may last up to four years in the Party-Mass Organization department of the Academy. The desire probably arises from a combination of ambition, self-interest and, for people from outside Bucharest, attraction to the relatively cosmopolitan life of the capital. Regardless of the cadre's desire, however, the insistence on such extensive political indoctrination constitutes a powerful institution of control to combat unwanted political changes relative to modernization/development.

From the background criteria mentioned thus far, one can construct a "model" Romanian sub-national political elite as a heuristic device. In a hypothetical case where a city has a vacancy in the Party secretariat and people's council permanent bureau, what would be a typical choice for a successor by the city-party bureau? As the county party bureau examines

122   DEMOCRATIC CENTRALISM IN ROMANIA

the city leaders' suggestions, what will be their criteria? Most likely, their choice will be someone who has most, and preferably all, of the following attributes (not necessarily in order of importance):

1) male
2) Romanian nationality
3) approximately 40 years of age
4) university degree in engineering, economics, or law
5) military service as an officer
6) U.T.C. member and leader while an adolescent and during university years
7) party activist while in military
8) cadre experience in low-level command positions in the economy, state, or socio-cultural organizations
9) party education at Ştefan Gheorghiu Academy
10) mid-level cadre position experience
11) member of local party committee

While these components of an individual's "background" are often necessary for becoming a sub-national political leader, they are not "sufficient." As long as nomenklatura operates, it is impossible to state that these criteria are, in fact, the only ones considered. It may be, for instance, that in some counties or lower levels, "social origin" and/or length of party membership remain the most important factors. I think not and suggest that differences among forty-two leaders' backgrounds were too small to compromise the uniformity in local elite recruitment.

Some overall "grasp" of criteria for elite recruitment is needed in order to relate background information to this study's test of a dialectical hypothesis. Notwithstanding the inaccuracies of a capsulization, the central party organs appear to have in mind the creation of a "communist intelligentsia"—a legion of cadre sufficiently specialized in all fields such that co-optation would no longer be required. Recruitment within the Party's ranks (i.e., a self-sufficiency) is the goal.

Such a characterization, however, fails to explain a phenomenon of that sort. When one begins to search for an explanation of changing elite recruitment in Romania, the possibilities for a dialectic approach become apparent.

Local Political Elites   123

The first "reason" for altered criteria is sub-national elite selection is
an endeavor closely akin to that which Stalin began in 1928. At the Soviet
Central Committee Plenum in July of that year a resolution was proclaim-
ed with the title "On Improving the Training of New Specialists." The
campaign inaugurated by that resolution was continued throughout the
early 1930s, ostensibly insisting on technological and administrative
competence for the CPSU's "command personnel."

Stalin's pronouncements during this period, if compared with quotations, cited earlier, from Ceauşescu, are strikingly similar. In 1931, for
instance, Stalin criticized the Bolsheviks for essentially the same reason
that Ceauşescu would criticize the PCR 41 years later:

> We not infrequently think that management signified merely sign-
> ing documents. This is a regrettable fact. It reminds one of Shched-
> rin's pompadours. You will remember how the lady told the young
> pompadour: "Don't bother your head about science, let others
> do that, it's none of your affair, your business is to manage and to
> sign documents." We must acknowledge to our shame that among
> us Bolsheviks there are not a few such people who conduct their
> business merely by signing papers.[135]

But in forcing the Party to pursue competency defined in technological
terms, Stalin was doing more; he was also forging a new tier of loyal
followers, replacing Lenin's Bolshevik cadre with his own, who would
be the means by which Stalin carried out the 1936-38 purges to eliminate
his opposition. In demanding that the CPSU have its own "intelligentsia,"
there was no doubt that it was to be an instrument for Stalin.

There is considerable evidence that Ceauşescu originally had a similar
motive for changing the criteria for political elite status. First, the Party
leader, in both cases, was in a not altogether secure position *vis-a-vis* other
men who had been associates of the previous leader. Second, in both cases,
development/modernization were closely linked to the leader's power and
prestige. Either of these similarities point to an impetus for changing
party cadre—to eliminate opposition elements under the guise of creating
more competent personnel, and to further the developmental/modern-
izing efforts with the influx of greater expertise. The important distinguishing feature, of course, is that the Romanian leadership, unlike Stalin,

DEMOCRATIC CENTRALISM IN ROMANIA

has been (since the mid-1950s at least) distinctly less inclined to use blatant coercive measures in the pursuit of dominance in the Party or the development/modernization.

What is "going on" in the local Romanian political elite, then, is partly an *induced* and uniformly applied change in the criteria for replenishing the Party ranks (remembering the exceptions in the case of sex and ethnic background). There exists a search, instituted from "the top," for cadre material, i.e., "command personnel," to direct and manage the Party-State apparatus in the increasingly complex Romanian society and economy inherent to development/modernization. In that sense, what is "going on" in the selection of new sub-national political elites is inseparable from the society and economy the Party directs.

Having said as much, however, we arrive at the second basic reason for changes in political elite selection. Although General Secretary Ceauşescu needed support in the Party, and more qualified local leaders would aid in the achievement of goals contributory to his position, there was another factor in the transition of local elites—a factor still present. As the Party began to aim Romania in the direction of autarkic policies, demanding industrialization, urbanization and higher productivity, the lack of competence on the part of local party and state officials charged with implementing Bucharest's policies became woefully apparent. The factory worker qua mayors, judges, et al. were, in the early and mid-1960s, "out of sync" with the tasks demanded of them. Vertical pressures within the Party, from the bottom up, constituted a warning that expectations existed that the Party too would conform to its own program.

Without oversimplification, the Party was required by its own membership in light of socio-economic change initiated by decisions from "the top," to (quite literally) "gear up" to the standards it had set for the rest of Romanian society. The Party's leadership's hand was forced on this issue, I would suggest, in order to keep the nomenklatura system operating in the realm of political appointments. The Party could not have, even if it had so desired, continued to appoint functionally incompetent people to sub-national political elite posts. The alternatives to change were either a return to overt coercion or the advent of challenges to the nomenklatura-type of elite replenishment. One might speculate that, for the Party as a whole, these were not pleasant alternatives.

Taken together, there are elements of a dialectical nature in these two reasons for altered elite recruitment criteria. It appears that the

Local Political Elites 125

central Party leadership wanted more competent sub-national political elites, but for its own reasons (as a quiescent purge and to expedite programs of development/modernization upon which the leadership's prestige was riding). But there was unwanted pressure from lower echelons, namely the mass party that was being ill-led by an older, dedicated, but relatively inept generation. One result of Ceauşescu's autarkic modernization/development program, then, has been ongoing escalation of the training, education, and expertise minimally needed to function as an effective local leader. In the late 1960s, it was to Ceauşescu's personal benefit (and coincidentally, Romania's) that a transition of party cadre was effected. From Gheorghiu-Dej associates such as Apostol, Stoica, and Draghici to the lowliest town and commune officials, the turnover was very significant, and the cult of Ceauşescu was seemingly insured.

But the key point antithetical to the regime's perspective is that the need for competence continues to grow and, even within the Party, the dissatisfaction with ineptitude is quite clear. One can imagine, then the dilemma for Ceauşescu and his associates; to accept and even appear to promote incremental change in the requirements for top sub-national positions, given that the Party will then retain its hold on appointments to posts of responsibility in political life, versus the suspicion that they have begun something which can no longer be controlled without coercive measures. In simplistic terms, national leaders surely want expertise, but they do not want to be pressured into wanting it. Moreover, Ceauşescu is unequivocally against incompetence (how could one favor it?), but certainly wants advice only when he asks for it.

C: GOAL-ORIENTATION OF SUB-NATIONAL POLITICAL ELITES

Romanian local political elites, although selected on the basis of what appear to be criteria applied uniformly across Romania, do not agree county to county or within counties with regard to goals and role perceptions. Simply put, while the Party maintains superficial uniformities in local political leadership, it has not succeeded in unifying the thought of such cadre. Others have made similar observations concerning the potential for conflict over public policy among communist elites:

126 DEMOCRATIC CENTRALISM IN ROMANIA

The setting of goals for society by the party and the prohibition of other channels through which the direction of society can be set, should not be taken to imply automatic commitment to these goals on the part of each individual in the Soviet Union. Nor does it mean that there are no differences over what these goals and directions should be . . . frictions and tensions, if not potential sources of conflict, have arisen at least *within* the party, if not between the party and the broader masses, over these fundamental questions.[136]

In this study, questions pertaining to the above-mentioned topics were asked of sub-national leaders during interviews. I was interested in two related but distinct phenomena—first, intra-national diversity of opinion among counties and, second, the degree of conflicting opinions within the political elite of each county relative to other counties. There were opportunities to gain insights into other matters as well, and such results will be mentioned in this section.

The first substantive question brought into elite interviews was, "What are the most important problems to be resolved by the Party and People's Council—in that locality—in the next 1-3 years?" In discussions which followed, I sought to find the parameters of problems mentioned, and to ascertain some details of the leadership's problem-solving efforts in that locale.

Three broad categories were used to classify responses—"economic," "political," and "socio-cultural." Although these concepts are not readily defined (for instance, when is an "economic problem" without "political" implications?), I found it usually possible to distinguish among responses emphasizing:

1) ideological commitment of citizens, maintenance of a socialist consciousness, democratization, increasing citizen involvement, bettering public administration, etc.;

2) heavy or light industry or agricultural production goals;

3) public service improvement (housing, water, roads), crime, urban planning, cultural awareness, etc.

Local Political Elites 127

I considered such kinds of problems mentioned as political, economic, and socio-cultural, respectively. Table XXI contains a simple tabulation of elites' answers.

TABLE XXI

Principal Local Problem as Indicated by Sub-National Political Elites

| Category of Answer | County | | | |
	Timiş	Cluj	Braşov	Iaşi
Economic	3	4	4	5
Political	1	0	2	2
Socio-Cultural	4	5	3	9

The table reveals, that among the few Timiş elites interviewed, the tendency was to indicate greatest conern for either economic or socio-cultural issues. Only one leader suggested "political" problems as the biggest issue facing his locale, with specific reference to the "ideological idealism" in the populace. That person, however, was also the one individual for whom the Party was a way of life—whose initial contacts with public issues had been in the early years of communist rule. That such a response was derived from this person suggests a relationship that I sense is a strong one, namely the connection between a local leader's concern for the political behavior (attitudes and actions) prevalent in his commune, city or county, and the circumstances under which he entered the sub-national political elite.

"Economic" problems to which reference was made included one case, in Timiş, where "agriculture and especially harvesting the crops" was the biggest concern for one leader at the commune level. Having said that, however, this particular member of the local political elite followed by noting that "next comes getting improvements in the town like running water into the homes and other urban developments." This position is one I found to be particularly characteristic of individuals elevated to the local elite in the 1960s under the impact of the transition to Ceauşescu's unchallenged dominance.[137]

128   DEMOCRATIC CENTRALISM IN ROMANIA

For instance, in a larger Timiş city, the economic problem was again cited as the major concern, specifically making economic development "more rapid and all-encompassing."[138] In that context, "all-encompassing" meant an egalitarian sense of reaching more people in the process of socio-economic development/modernization. The proposed solution to this local problem was intriguing, as this leader asserted that he and his fellow elites were "desirous of making things competitive to encourage this process."[139] Asked to explain his use of the word "competitive," the subject began by distinguishing his proposals to solve local needs from "capitalist competition" by asserting the existence of "socialist competition" whereby the only goal is to "do a better job than another."[140]

Notwithstanding such definitional back-tracking, one should note that a "solution" of the type he suggested is the essence of the *problem* mentioned by the leader quoted earlier (i.e., a problem of political attitude). One local elite's problem, therefore, was closely akin, if not identical to, solutions suggested by another.

Also in Timiş, I spoke with local political elites whose primary concern was the "quality of life" in their locale, expressed in socio-cultural terms. For instance, an important party/state official in Timişoara answered the general question about local problems this way:

If you drive around Timişoara, I'm sure you will see the problems. Although we have made tremendous progress in the last two decades, we will have not solved some basic ones (problems) like paving roads, getting running water in all the homes, assuring adequate electrical supply, etc. Although these are almost overcome, we will have residual difficulties. For now and the future, you will see we have too many people for the houses we can provide, and this problem is made worse by the people from rural communities who try to sneak into the city. Being a border city, too, we incur problems of the black market and small illegalities that other Romanian cities do not face.[141]

That kind of exposition by a local political elite is not at all in concert with opinions of other leaders within the same county in Romania. Beyond mere differences in priorities, these positions connote opposing

Local Political Elites   129

goals for society and, therefore, contrary tasks for the polity. Surely, differences of opinion within the confines of the Party are likely to be found in all communist states, yet, in this case, one must keep in mind that these contrary opinions arise in one small region of a communist-party state among the political elite, who were selected on the basis of uniform criteria. Were we to exclude cases of elites recruited prior to the Ceauşescu period (in Timiş only two people of eight interviewed), large differences of opinion remain apparent.

One must be aware, of course, that it is problematic to infer "conflict" from "differences of opinion" when the most obvious evidence for the former (overt debate, competitive election campaigns, contentious editorial comment in the media, etc.) are proscribed in a communist party state. Yet, I am convinced that the positions taken by these elites are *not* merely different orderings of priorities based upon their professional interests. Instead, elites with whom I spoke seemed to suggest alternative interpretations of what a Socialist government *ought* to do. In other words, local elites were fundamentally divided regarding their prescriptions for, and evaluation of, goals for the communist regime. I do not mean to suggest that *national* elites have divergent opinions or, even if they did diverge, that the regime would be in serious difficulty. Nevertheless, the contrasts I heard were not those of minor differences in social priorities.

After recognizing the existence of inherent conflict regarding public policy, I sought further elaboration in other counties when the same question was asked. In Cluj, for instance, a number of replies emphasized public services, provisioning of food supplies, etc., all related to the standard of living in that area. Typical of that position was this statement:

> We have some twenty million lei with which we need to modernize the market area. But we have long had the plans ready for a six floor shopping store. But 10,000,000 more lei are needed for that project. . . also the provisioning of our city is our constant problem. Commerce is our "Achilles heel." Other cities, it seems, are always better provided. . . . [142]

In Cluj County, no elites were interviewed who evinced a clearly "political issue-orientation, and opinions such as the one above were about equally divided with those having an "economic" (i.e., industrual) focus.

130 DEMOCRATIC CENTRALISM IN ROMANIA

Responses in Timiş and Cluj were much alike. Opinins on public policy issues exhibited inherent conflict in both counties, but the differences were largely confined to the continuum between economic versus socio-cultural concerns. Between Braşov and Iaşi counties, however, opinions seemed to differ more starkly. Reasons for making such an assessment can best be explained through examples.

In a Braşov commune, for instance, leaders focused on the very practical problems related to their community's standard of living—bringing running water into the homes, continuing educational improvements, and street paving.[143] The similar, but more sophisticated, viewpoint of a city first vice-president was as follows:

We must take an integral view of all the city's problems—they can't be divided in actuality. In theory, I suppose you could say we have social problems, with many subdivisions, and problems of people, also with many subdivisions. Socially, systematization has received great emphasis since Comrade Ceauşescu came here, and we finalized a plan of constructing social buildings such as schools and hospitals. But many more social problems arise from industrialization, the goal of our country. We lack sufficient public transportation for the peak hours, water is critically short, electricity is low, and other problems arise because of our advancing industrialization. Even getting rid of waste is a problem with growing population and industry.[144]

Socio-cultural concerns, in the above quotation, stand in contrast to "industrialization"... a focus for public policy that seemed to come under veiled criticism when this elite cited "more social problems" that "arise from industrialization." But such a position was a minority in Braşov county. Just as often, I heard that more industry was the center of attention for local political elites:

We have made Braşov the biggest truck and tractor building site in the country, established a large ball-bearing factory, and made Braşov a center of light industry...it is imperative that we continue and expand this within the context of the Five Year Plan.[145]

Moreover, representatives of a distinctly "hard-line" view are expressive in their concerns at the county and city level:

Local Political Elites   131

. . . a strong socialist mentality [and] commitment to the goals
of Comrade Ceauşescu are required of all citizens. . . we must
strive through our schools and propaganda to further such goals.[146]

Elites interviewed in Iaşi county also answered by taking different
positions along the continuum I have suggested, but with a stronger
socio-cultural focus than in other counties. To be sure, Iaşi's leadership
gave opinions over a spectrum equally as wide as Braşov elites—for instance, those that emphasized economic issues:

[Our problems are] mostly economic in nature. We're trying to
change to greater industrial production, and towards zootechnic
production (a commune leader).[147]

Economic development occupied our greatest attention—which
new industries will come to town, how to get materials for these
industries, etc. We're constantly doing analyses of these problems
. . . (a city leader).[148]

Economic problems. . . diversification of production in accord
with last year's normative act. We must worry about coordinating
local development with national economic plans, and about modernization (mechanization) in agriculture (a county leader.)[149]

Yet, within the same county—indeed, sometimes, within the same city
—opinions were apparent that contrasted sharply with those of an economic nature; for example:

Continued urbanization [is our principal problem]. . . we have a
plan until 1980. . . we have a problem with transportation, for
example, because of a huge increase in population. Then, housing
and building remain problems for the same reason. . . . [150]

Our biggest problem is that of public services (gospodarea municipal); housing and material assistance to schools are certainly as
important.[151]

Such statements were the most common types of responses among interviewed leaders in Iaşi and constituted a larger proportion of anwers than
in other counties.

132   DEMOCRATIC CENTRALISM IN ROMANIA

Nevertheless, there were representative "hard-line" positions taken by a small number of subjects, wherein the leader specified political issues as his main concern:

As you know, in a socialist state such as ours, we must always be striving to build a truly communist society. This is our goal—our daily task—not only in the next few years, but always.[152]

These quotations, taken together suggest the parameters of intra-elite conflict to which Table XXI alluded. While one must accept the possibility that these data are not wholly representative because of an unavoidably small sample, responses did replicate each other from county to county. At the least, then, evidence exists to indicate a lack of unity among subnational elites; there *is* diversity of opinion regarding what needs to be done. More importantly, one might infer that directives from Bucharest do not cause local leaders to agree on foci for their attention.

If local political elites in Romania disagree over the immediate problems facing them, then they disagree in similar ways. Again and again one finds certain kinds of problem "areas" being mentioned that I have denoted as political, economic, and socio-cultural. In other words, there is a pattern to the way local deaders disagree with counties differing only slightly as to the central tendency of elite responses.

If one codes the problem "areas" of political, economic, and socio-cultural with scores of 1, 2, and 3, respectively, and multiplies those by the frequency of occurrence in each county, a mean score can be obtained. These means are:

Timiş	2.38
Cluj	2.56
Braşov	2.11
Iaşi	2.44

These numbers imply that Braşov elites, from the most developed/modernized region of the four counties, were somewhat less inclined to cite socio-cultural problems (coded 3) as principal concerns. The other counties, scoring quite close to one another, are not easily differentiated. Given that the Iaşi sample was larger, however, we can most confidently

Local Political Elites

contrast Braşov with Iaşi and note the slightly greater emphasis on the latter county on issues related to the quality of life.

Although these suspicions require testing on a wider scale, one must assume that the Party's central leadership desires more, not less, consensus as to concerns for local political elites. Very likely they would be further desirous of a focus on economic issues. Given such assumptions, Bucharest may not be altogether happy with either the diversity of opinion or the tendencies therein.

We can say with some assurance that local elites are not of one mind across Romania or within one county. Conflict is implicit when the attitudes of local leaders are at variance with each other and with central party organs. When one leader's "solution" is a "problem" in the eyes of another, a reasonable presumption is that such implicit conflict eventually manifests itself in explicit competition within the local party apparatus, as well as in the context of competition for resources distributed from Bucharest.

Making such decisions about the distribution of resources, when people do not agree, involves the conflict or competition inherent to all politics, whether in communist states or not. An example of this conflict was observed when a commune permanent bureau met, and the issue of a "cultural house" as opposed to agricultural machinery was brought up. The relative values of both were argued by spokesmen and a decision was "announced" by the chairman to which all assented (even though some peoples' votes seemed paradoxical given their stated positions); the decision was to build the cultural facility, but to use revenues from it in its first years of operation for additional mechanization.

To summarize, if conflicts within the political elite grow as Romania becomes more developed/modernized, support would be evident for a dialectical approach to politics in such a system. Additional research at another point in time is needed to ascertain any change in the diversity of opinion. More immediately, however, we have the suspicion that a higher rate of change from lower socio-economic levels may be related to a shift of elite opinion away from political and economic orientations towards socio-cultural concerns.

134 DEMOCRATIC CENTRALISM IN ROMANIA

C: ROLE PERCEPTIONS OF SUB-NATIONAL ELITES

The implication arises from a dialectical hypothesis that the *role* of political leaders in developing/modernizing states changes contrary to the intentions of leaders themselves; having initiated and directed massive social and economic transformations, political elites (as a group and as individuals) are drawn into different roles. These "different roles" one might suppose, would be willingly assumed by some—probably the elites recruited once sustained development/modernization was underway—while others who had occupied leadership posts earlier would be under some pressure to adapt. This does not necessarily imply an attitudinal change, but does connote a necessary change in "style" of leadership, conforming as it were to "the times."

Such preliminary speculation is not without basis in observable behavior, in Romania and elsewhere. Indeed, Lucian Pye has suggested that for countries where the elite is closed, "if leadership has any success in advancing development, the elite culture will have to *make some accommodations to the masses*," and hence he suggests that an "identity crisis is likely to change at an early stage to conform" to a "restrictive elite culture."[153] At the national level in Romania, Ceauşescu had himself adopted a "new style," according to one observer, which reflects an "emphasis on modernism," as "he tries to recognize and to accommodate new trends wherever they may appear." Moreover, elements of Charles de Gaulle's style, "such as the 'immersion in the masses' technique," have been "integrated into Ceauşescu's pattern of public behavior" in the opinion of the same analyst.[154]

My own observations tend to confirm that assessment. During times when Ceauşescu is not traveling abroad, he makes strenuous efforts to visit all corners of Romania in the company of other central party notables. Care is taken to photograph the Party General Secretary with national and local leaders at factories, schools, and in the fields with the agricultural workers. These forays into the countryside are not "whistle-stop campaigning" per se, but it is tempting to find an analogue to the style of Romanian leadership in the 1970s in the efforts typical of candidates in contested elections. Clearly, local leaders cannot but see Ceauşescu's behavior as an example for them to follow.

The counter-argument is twofold; first, there is no evidence that what Ceauşescu does is what local leaders do—i.e., that shaking hands and

Local Political Elites   135

kissing babies might be the General Secretary's behavior, but we have no
cause to generalize and, second, were it a general kind of leadership
behavior, there is no reason to presume that it is antithetical to the Party's
desires. Moreover, perhaps Nicolae Ceauşescu *enjoys* public contact no
less than populists of an American genre.

To the latter point, one cannot argue knowledgably since no confidant
of Ceauşescu's is likely to publish memoirs soon. There can be little
doubt, however, that for even the most casual observer of local politics
in Romania, that at all sub-national levles the example of the Party Chairman is taken seriously. Studious effort was made by county leaders in
Iaşi, for example, to tour areas damaged by excessive soil erosion and mud
slides and to assure the public of governmental measures to assist people
and to prevent a recurrence.[155] In cities, high party/state officials regularly made personal appearance at factories, construction sites, schools,
etc. Additionally, at every level, the possibility of an individual citizen
addressing himself to a local leader has been preserved in "audiences"
which all sub-national political elites are obliged to conduct once a week.

All this implies a considerable amount of elite-public contact at the
present time. A typical day for a commune first vice-president, for instance, includes several of the forms of contact mentioned above:

> . . . the morning begins for me at about seven A.M. with citizens'
> complaints (from letters and by 'phone), after which I leave the
> office to tour construction sites. After that I usually come back
> here in the late morning to review plans, order new acquisitions,
> etc. In the afternoon, It's usually more complaints, and needs of
> citizens, particularly in the audiences, which are once a week.[156]

The key question remains, however, "is this contrary to the Party's intentions?" If institutionalized contact such as audiences, tours of public
facilities, inspections of storm damage, or encouragement given to peasants
involved in harvesting, are activities of communist elites necessitatted by
their goals of development/modernization, but the antithesis of their
desire, this could be construed as part of a "dialectic."

Notwithstanding the importance of such a question, it is impossible
to assess the "desires" of "intentions" of all sub-national elites. One
can presume that, among the hundreds of local leaders, not all are eager
to become truly public figures. Furthermore, among those who might be

DEMOCRATIC CENTRALISM IN ROMANIA

so inclined, any feeling of being pressured to do so would be a source of irritation. This was evident on several occasions:

> Generally . . . people are more pretentious and they demand more and more . . . we are not overworked, but all employees *must* satisfy the people.[157]

Another city leader also expressed irritation prior to conducting an audience:

> It is difficult to understand why people complain about so much today—and such trivial things.[158]

I am unsure as to how widespread such sentiments are. That some local leaders are preforming taks out of requirements tends to suggests, I think, implicit political role conflict dialectically related to social and economic changes.

Thus far I have indicated several reasons for believing that role conflict does exist among local political elites in Romania. Overall, the standards of autocratic leadership, long the norm in communist party states, appear to have been challenged by a new "style"—a model adopted by Party General Secretary Ceauşescu that has pressured local elites to "go public" as well.

But to leave this issue here would give rise to an incomplete understanding of the complex world in which sub-national leaders live in a developing/modernizing communist party state. If a dialectical hypothesis is correct, then we must look not only to conflict between local levels and the central apparatus over the role of sub-national leaders, but also to other planes of conflict concerning how local elites ought to behave. Inevitably, there are contradictory indications for any one sub-national leader as to precisely how he sould play the role. For reasons I will clarify below, I have assigned labels to four "models" that present-day local Romanian elites might see before them:

1)	the autocrat
2)	the oligarch
3)	the expert
4)	the populist

Local Political Elites 137

On the one hand, there is the momentum of twenty or more years when local leaders were autocrats in their own right, secreting themselves in party sessions, largely invisible and unkown to the general public, making few if any attempts to legitimize actions through people's councils. In the 1970s this model has little overt support, and most party secretaries seek to surround themselves in at least the appearance of a collective leadership—i.e., an oligarchy. In such a circumstance, one many may still rule, but he rules through persuasion and personality, and might be overruled by others in the local political elite.[159]

Another model exists that is more recent. Since the late 1960s, new cadre recruited to be local leaders cannot fail to recognize one of the bases for their own advancement—namely, technical or administrative expertise. There is a tendency for some political elites to seek a role confined to his expertise. But specialization, alone, does not solve local leaders' dilemmas, nor unify their perceptions of what they ought to be doing (as was indicated in answers to the first question regarding principal local problems). In other words, the model of an "expert" is imprecise. For some leaders, the increasingly universal criterion of specialization connotes an insulated political elite, while for others the advanced education might broaden their viewpoints (e.g., to include more concern for socio-cultural issues and/or to suggest increased contact with the public). Very likely then, conflicting interpretations of leadership roles exist within the cohort of new cadre.

For want of a better term, I have used the word "populist" to denote a fourth model that seemed present among sub-national elites—the kind of leader who genuinely enjoyed the public contact, who appeared to covet popular appeal, and whose own personality and convictions demanded overt displays of concern for public welfare and "consumerism."[160] There are expectations by the populace that create for all local leaders a "populist" model, which either looms as a spectre or exists as an opportunity, depending upon a leader's personality, abilities, and the constraints imposed by party leaders directly above. These expectations brought more than one interviewed elite to label citizens as "pretentious." Many of the newest leaders, however, accept these norms (witness the apparent widespread concern for problems related to the standard of living cited earlier).

These "models" exist only as typologies, of course, and it is unlikely that any individual local political elite could be categorized as one or the

other. But if no one person fits into these classifications, they they can be used to advantage in combinations. A description of Ceauşescu using these categories, for example, could be that of an "autocratic populist," derived from the cult of personality he insists upon and his penchant for public contact. That the General Secretary might be accurately described as to his leadership style in such terms indicates the conflicting "signals" local leaders must receive; autocracy and populism, if not exact opposites, at least contain elements of each other's antithesis, hence implying a dialectic in leadership that exhibits some of both traits.

For sub-national Romanian leadership the situation is similar. Choices between or among the so-called "models" for leadership roles involve conflicts along various planes—with the central apparatus, with other local elites who have different functional specialties, with citizen expectations and demands, or a combination of these.

Any person involved in political leadership where the position he or she occupied is not institutionally defined, but instead is subject to the grossly differing models I have suggested, will be involved in conflict. Again, in a communist party state, this conflict is not always observable. In order to gain some empirical evidence of this phenomenon, however, interviews included questions related to the perception of roles by local leaders.

Confusion over leadership roles (how to behave) adds to and creates forms of conflict that are antithetical to a communist party regime such as conflict among the local political elites in one county, and conflict between local leaders and their constituency. In both cases, these forms of role conflict are detrimental to the efficiency for which the regime strives, given its goal of development/modernization. Clearly, if that very goal of socio-economic change has as one by-product the promotion of conflict over how elites ought to behave, *then* such evidence would support a dialectical approach.

Interviews produced some indications that conflict between local leaders and citizens is increasing, and that local elites and the Party's central apparatus conflict, but only insofar as sub-national leaders petition for changes in resource allocation because they disagree with decisions. In such contexts, the four counties were not markedly distinct from one another. Yet I also found that Iaşi exhibited more intra-elite conflict (that is, the elites themselves were less united) about their leadership roles than in Braşov, (but less different from Timiş and Cluj).

Local Political Elites 139

These generalizations are, in part, based on one question that elicited interesting replies—simply, "Are you a politician?" My goal was to obtain answers that could help me interpret how elites perceived their role as a local leader. Responses, of course, were not only direct outputs of role perception, but were also indicative of an elite's interpretation of the term "politician." Results of this question are presented below.

TABLE XXII

Local Political Elites' Responses to Question: "Are you a politician?"

Category of Answer		Timiş	Cluj	Braşov	Iaşi
Yes					
a)	Seeks public support	1	2	1	5
b)	Inherent to public life	1	1	1	1.5
No					
c)	Civil servant	3	3	2	4
d)	Leading citizen	–	1	–	–
e)	Party activist	–	.5	2	2.5
f)	Party servant	2	1.5	2	3
No Answer		1	–	1	–

A simple "yes" or "no" answer, I found, told little of how an elite perceived his leadership role. In the case of an affirmative response, one kind of "yes" (b) was, in fact, a denial that a leadership position meant public contact; since all economic and social activity is political (or so I was told), any leader is inherently a "politician." By this way of thinking, one is a "politician" because of a leadership role, not vice versa. In a Iaşi commune, a mayor (who is scored as .5 in both category (b) and (a) exemplified this position:

Always; anyone who said otherwise would not have a conscience. The mayor must be a party leader, and he must always be concerned with the political education of others.[161]

140   DEMOCRATIC CENTRALISM IN ROMANIA

Conversely, people who answered "yes" in another sense (a) implied that their position rested on the cooperation and support received from the community as a whole, which is quite distinct from the other way of responding affirmatively. One commune mayor (party chairman), again in Iaşi county, answered without hesitation for instance: "Certainly . . . I must always seek to help the people, and with that help things have changed."[162] A city vice-president in Iaşi county also answered in that vein:

Absolutely. I came into government by my own will. Politics in Romania, for me, is the transposition of the interests of the people into action and laws.[163]

Follow-up questions were also asked when the initial response was negative. Answers fell into four categories ((c) through (f)). Often the subject would provide an answer as did a city first vice-president in Iaşi, by simply saying that he considered himself "more a civil servant than a politician."[164] That statement was very much like the position taken by a city people's council secretary in Timiş who answered "no," explaining that his work in civic planning as a civil engineer brought him "inevitably" into a political role.[165] Other elites also denied that they were "politicians" by relating their role to the Party (an activist or a servant or closely related synonyms). "I was elected to do the work of the Party" went a fairly typical response of the last (f) category, while another leader answered negatively by referring to himself as one of the Party "activ," leading "the politically conscious mass" in his city.[166]

These different ways of answering "yes" or "no" to my question suggest that there is, first, considerable diversity about what roles local leaders ought to play (or at least, what roles an American researcher should be told they perform). More than that, however, there seems to have been relatively ideological ways to answer both yes and no, and relatively moderate ways to do the same. Given that possibility, I elected to designate responses (b), (e), and (f) as the more "hard-line" responses, and (a), (c), and (d) as relatively moderate answers. The underlying assumption is that role perceptions emphasizing the public, civic responsibility, citizenship, etc., represent a different state of mind than do answers which imply that public contact is derived from a position of

Local Political Elites   141

power, not the inverse, and which focus on the Party as a definer of
roles.

When tabulated, using the groupings suggested above, a county to
county comparison was possible.

	Timiş	Cluj	Braşov	Iaşi	Total
Moderate	4	6	3	9	22
Hard-line	3	3	5	7	18
Ratio	1.3	2.0	.6	1.3	

The ratio of one kind of answer to another suggests that Braşov's leaders
gave what one might judge to be more orthodox answers. There is no
clear-cut dichotomy between Braşov and Iaşi here—indeed, Cluj leaders
apparently see their roles in a more moderate light. But Braşov's low
ratio in the above comparison might be important in the context of this
study. Braşov leaders, it seems, tended to say that they were or were not
"politicians" in ways implying greater ideological and party commitment.
Were that true, then Braşov's high level of development/modernization
is unlikely to be a key to any dialectic since greater ideological and party
commitment are clearly not antithetical results.

Comparing counties purely on the basis of "yes" and "no" replies is
another way of trying to measure similarities and differences. If one
were to make such a comparison on a percentage basis, other contrasts
are apparent:

	Timiş	Cluj	Braşov	Iaşi	Total
Yes	25%	33%	22%	41%	30%
No	63%	67%	66%	59%	65%
No Response	13%	——	11%	——	5%

Here we find Iaşi county to be most obviously different from other
locations, having a higher proportion of affirmative answers, and Braşov
the lowest. Despite a small sample, the difference between Braşov and
Iaşi responses gives some credence to the hypothesis that development/
modernization have political implications. Perhaps more important, there
is a plausible suggestion here for further study—namely, that faster changes
from relatively lower starting points on any socio-economic scale may

142 DEMOCRATIC CENTRALISM IN ROMANIA

imply different political behavior (in the sense of leaders' role perceptions) than do slower changes from more advanced "levels."

Merely answering "yes" to the aforementioned question, of course, cannot necessarily be interpreted as the antithesis of how Ceauşescu himself might have answered the same question. Thus, the methods for intercounty comparison must be viewed together, and their mutual implications considered.

Given that both ways of arriving at inter-county comparisons finds Braşov lowest of the four subject counties, a reasonable conclusion would be that local leaders there are fairly unified in having inclinations to see themselves as public figures and in a tendency to have role perceptions focusing on the Party and its ideology. Iaşi leaders, however, provided less consistent responses such that more elites answered affirmatively (i.e., that they did see themselves as politicians), while Iaşi does not have as high a "moderate/hard-line" ratio as did Cluj county. Partially from this inconsistency, but more from my own discussions with Iaşi elites, I believe role conflict among local leaders is much more prevalent in Iaşi county than in Braşov, with Timiş and Cluj counties midway between them.

One statistical treatment of these data that suggests a similar conclusion is the Rice Index of Cohesion, a long-employed measure agreement in roll calls.[167] This index is obtained by simply finding the absolute difference between the percentages answering "yes" and "no" for each county. The lower the resultant number, then, the closer were the proportions of "yes" and "no" replies, implying least cohesion. Braşov scores highest with 44, and Timiş at 38, Cluj with 34, and Iaşi scoring 18 follows. Hence. from this index, Braşov seems the most cohesive in leadership role perception, Iaşi the least.

Unfortunately, the instruments of measurement used here are not sufficiently refined, nor was the sample sufficiently large, to derive stronger evidence. Nevertheless, we have reason to suspect that rapid changes such as the development/modernization desired by the Party are, at least, coincident with an increase in the disunity among local elites over their leadership roles. This relationship should, then, be investigated in further research.

Local Political Elites   143

E. SUMMARY

Sub-national political elites, specifically members of people's council permanent bureaus and/or the Party bureau, have been examined in this chapter through interview data. The backgrounds of local leaders implied that changes were effected by the Ceauşescu regime sometime in the mid-to-late 1960s regarding the criteria for entry into the sub-national political elite. For purposes of his own power *vis-a-vis* competitors, as well as the prestige invested in his autarkic goals, Ceauşescu inaugurated a major shift in sub-national elite replenishment. At the same time, the organization of Romania's territorial-administrative units and their state organs was accomplished.

But from the General Secretary's own speeches, and the concern for indoctrination of cadres demonstrated by his revitalization of the Party's educational facilities, it seems clear that the 1970s brought the recognition that altering criteria for elite status had become a *process* rather than a one-time event. Although the Party's central apparatus can and does still operate a nomenklatura system that imposes a superficial uniformity on criteria for new elites, the evolution of attitudes has been ongoing—perhaps in directions antithetical to the regime's designs.

Those attitudes were measured in two principal directions—the goal orientation of a particular leader and his role perception. While the technique of measurement was not refined nor the sample large, some broad implications were nevertheless evident.

Most clearly, local leaders do not agree. There are considerable differences across Romania and within any single county as to what issues are most important and what are proper leadership roles. At the least, differing opinions of these kinds are contrary to the ideals of an ideologically-based, self-proclaimed vanguard; if these elites are politically "conscious," they are evidently conscious of different goals and needs in their locale and different models for their own behavior.

In a communist party state, such conflict, or disagreement, can be construed as evidence that a dialectic is operative. Leaders, after all, are to a Marxist-Leninist the most progressive elements of society among whom divisive interests have been removed. As guides for society's transition to communism, they logically cannot be pointing in different directions. But the Romanian sub-national leaders are doing precisely that—they

144   DEMOCRATIC CENTRALISM IN ROMANIA

disagree on what they ought to be doing and how they should be doing it—and that disagreement appears to be somehow fostered by the development/modernization pursued by the Party.

Morten Gorden, in an insightful work on conflict management in a comparative perspective makes the point that "progressive spokesmen" (i.e., leaders in states where an ideological party dominates) "speak for that body of ideas, usually codified in an ideology, that provides the guides for action."[168] Gorden continues:

> Highly correlated with such progressive notions is the sense that the spokesmen should be unitary . . . *the elite is expected to be a unified one* . . . *but such unity is increasingly difficult to achieve* . . . *the demands of economic growth have forced a measure of decentralization* on the economic units. A new set of spokesmen is forming in the Soviet Union and Eastern Europe. They tend to be pragmatic types with values that maximize growth rather than the Good Book.[169] (emphasis added).

Gorden's points are well taken, if seen in the light of interview results discussed in this chapter. We have seen substantial evidence that subnational elites are neither united in their goal or issue orientation nor in their role perception. That lack of unity among leadership can be, itself, antithetical to the regime's intentions as Gorden implies. Moreover, replies in elite interviews encourage the belief (albeit a tenuous one) that Iași leaders lean towards socio-cultural concerns and more often identify themselves as "politicians," while Brașov leaders come closest to focusing on economic goals and least accept the title of "politician." While the Iași-Brașov contrast did not firmly hold in other respects, the attitudinal differences among local leaders often correspond to rates of socio-economic change.

CONCLUSION

Hypotheses regarding political life in the midst of changing social and economic conditions offer the recognition that the political decision to develop and/or modernize connotes political results often antithetical to the regime pursuing such goals. Having aimed initially to test such dialectical hypotheses in a communist party state, an assessment of the possibilities for such an approach to politics in developing/modernizing states can now be undertaken.

Development/modernization as co-extensive processes are not uniform throughout Romania. There are, in the case of four counties studied here, differentiated socio-economic levels as measured by a number of convential indices. More important, the *rates* of change (presumably changes one could label as development/modernization) are unequal. Indeed, the four counties' rates of change are inversely ranked as compared with their socio-economic levels. Braşov, clearly the district with the highest standard of living, changes most slowly; Iaşi, where the levels of most indices are lowest, is changing most rapidly.

In that alone, there is nothing to suggest antithetical results of socio-economic change. Indeed, such conclusions only serve to suggest the genuine efforts by a centralized regime to spread available wealth more evenly—i.e., to raise the less advanced regions to a more equitable position *vis-a-vis* more well-to-do districts.

The question is, however, whether or not such internal contrasts co-vary with political changes at sub-national levels. Towards that question, later chapters in this study were directed. In both Chapters IV and

145

DEMOCRATIC CENTRALISM IN ROMANIA

V, aspects of local political life were examined in search of evidence to support or disprove the hypothesis of a dialectical relationship between socio-economic and political changes.

These efforts were made more difficult by the problem of periodicity as well as small samples. It follows that interpretations of results necessarily fall into the category of tendency statements, with empirical verification sometimes failing to achieve statistical significance. Notwithstanding some healthy skepticism, it remains plausible to accept certain broadly-based findings suggested in Chapters IV and V.

From a questionnaire orally administered to deputies, the essential diversity of local politics was established by many items; between counties or within one county, these actors at various sub-national levels neither think nor behave as one. Measured in terms of differences among the four subject counties, diversity was noted in the case of questions that sought background characteristics of people's council deputies.

The earliest political involvement and dates of party membership were found, for example, in Braşov, while Iaşi deputies gave indications of more recent beginnings to political involvement and later party membership. Subsequent questions, however, suggested that Iaşi deputies were more active outside the Party and/or were more often politically inexperienced prior to becoming deputies than council members in other counties. Current organizational membership mirrored deputies' precouncil activities in that Iaşi responses implied the highest level of nonparty involvement at the time when research was conducted. Braşov council members indicated that both before and after their election as deputies they saw political involvement in terms of the Party more than deputies in the other three counties.

Attitudes reflect intra-national diversity as well, often in similar patterns. Several questions, for instance, revealed that Iaşi deputies regularly mentioned more problems for the local people's council and a wider range of such problems. Moreover, Iaşi deputies were somewhat less reluctant to suggest substantive changes in people's councils, cited more ostensibly non-political organizations in their locale that attempted to influence public policies, and referred not to the Party but to their own skills and expertise as the reason for their selection as deputy candidates.

From such tendencies, we can tentatively infer that actors in local politics from the locale with lowest socio-economic levels, but which is

Conclusion 147

changing most rapidly, have backgrounds and opinions that adhere less to the Party than deputies from areas where change is slower, but socio-economic levels are higher. Such co-variance, of course, says nothing about causality. But the possibility that a dialectic approach might be a valid way to analyze politics in developing states gains credence through such associations. While overt manifestations of dialectical processes are muted in closed political systems, conflict between the Communist Party and the opinions of deputies in places like Iaşi county seems implicit.

Interviews conducted with local political elites again revealed the considerable diversity of backgrounds and opinions, although recent patterns of elite replenishment have followed a rather consistent "form-ula" that is now reducing background differences. But opinions are, quite clearly, not as unified as one might conjecture for governmental leaders in an ideologically-based political system. Diversity among opin-ions could be viewed, alone as part of a dialectic. The specific nature of county-to-county differences, however, implied that a county's rate of socio-economic change co-varies with changes in elite attitudes—that is, the more rapidly changing, the greater the concern noticed for "socio-cultural" issues, while changing less rapidly appears to coincide with a greater concern for "political" and "economic" issues. Also from inter-views, the rapidity of modernizing or developmental changes was found to be coincident with greater disunity among the elites with respect to role perceptions.

For the most part, socio-economic *levels* seemed inversely related to opinions or behavior that might be antithetical in the regime's perspective. In other words, where change is slow in a relatively advanced socio-economic environment, the Party seems to have a more secure foothold (to include earlier recruitment and party membership as indicated by the deputy questionnaire). Were subsequent research to consider the dialecti-cal hypothesis again, rates of change, not levels, appear to be the key form of the independent variable to test.

If these measurements accurately portrary sub-national politics in a developing communist party state, then changes inaugurated by the Party to strengthen itself may threaten to exceed the capacities of the Party to control them.[170] A dialectical hypothesis appears, in light of this study, to point in a fruitful direction by suggesting that massive socio-economic changes called modernization/development begin to

148   DEMOCRATIC CENTRALISM IN ROMANIA

politicize, educate, and mobilize the populace, leading to demands on,
and conflict within, the political system. We have seen evidence, albeit
unavoidably limited, that such conflict and demands grow instead of
diminish where socio-economic change is pursued most rapidly.

It does not follow that the regime of Nicolae Ceauşescu or communist
rule in Romania faces its own demise by continuing to push for develop-
ment/modernization. If research discovered signs that political decisions
seeking to "rearrange reality" yield some antithetical results, this study
also pointed to aspects of local politics still manipulated by the national
leadership and those sub-national leaders tied to the status quo.

A nomenklatura system, while it apparently fails to assure that posts
of responsibility are filled with people who think alike, can and is employed to force certain criteria upon sub-national levels for entry into
important positions. Moreover, the setting, procedures, and issues at
people's council sessions and meetings of political elites remain quite
uniform. There is no reason to suspect that party control will soon diminish in such respects. Such control, in combination with judicious flexi-
bility, are sources for the regime's continued vitality.

Even without overt coercion, then, communist party regimes have
mechanisms at their disposal to constrain political change. Yet, Ceauşescu's remarks and actions of the late 1960s and early 1970s imply
that the national leadership feared that their control mechanisms were
not achieving desired ends, and that care would have to be exercised
in order to channel the thought as well as the observable behavior of
actors in local politics. Antithetical results of politically determined
change, then, must have been apparent not too many years after Gheorghiu-Dej and then Ceauşescu opted for massive industrialization and
urbanization.

But most socialists and communists begin with, as one observer states,
"an almost supernatural" faith in their techniques of social and economic
transformation, believing that their organizational capabilities, and particularly the Party's control of state organs, will assure control of change.[171]
The Romanian regime, it would seem, no longer shares that faith, having
learned in less dramatic fashion the lessons of orthodox communists
in Poland, Hungary, and Czechoslovakia.

Conclusion 149

Ceaușescu now realizes that principally as a result of efforts to develop/modernize, sub-national political life is involved in a transitional stage, where "the interaction between . . . ideological goals and the requirements of the social system . . . will generate a process that in time modifies both the ideology and the reality" of socio-economic life that the Party initially set out to change.[172] Ceaușescu's dilemma is to see that the outcome of such a dialectical process is within tolerable limits for a communist party regime.

APPENDICES

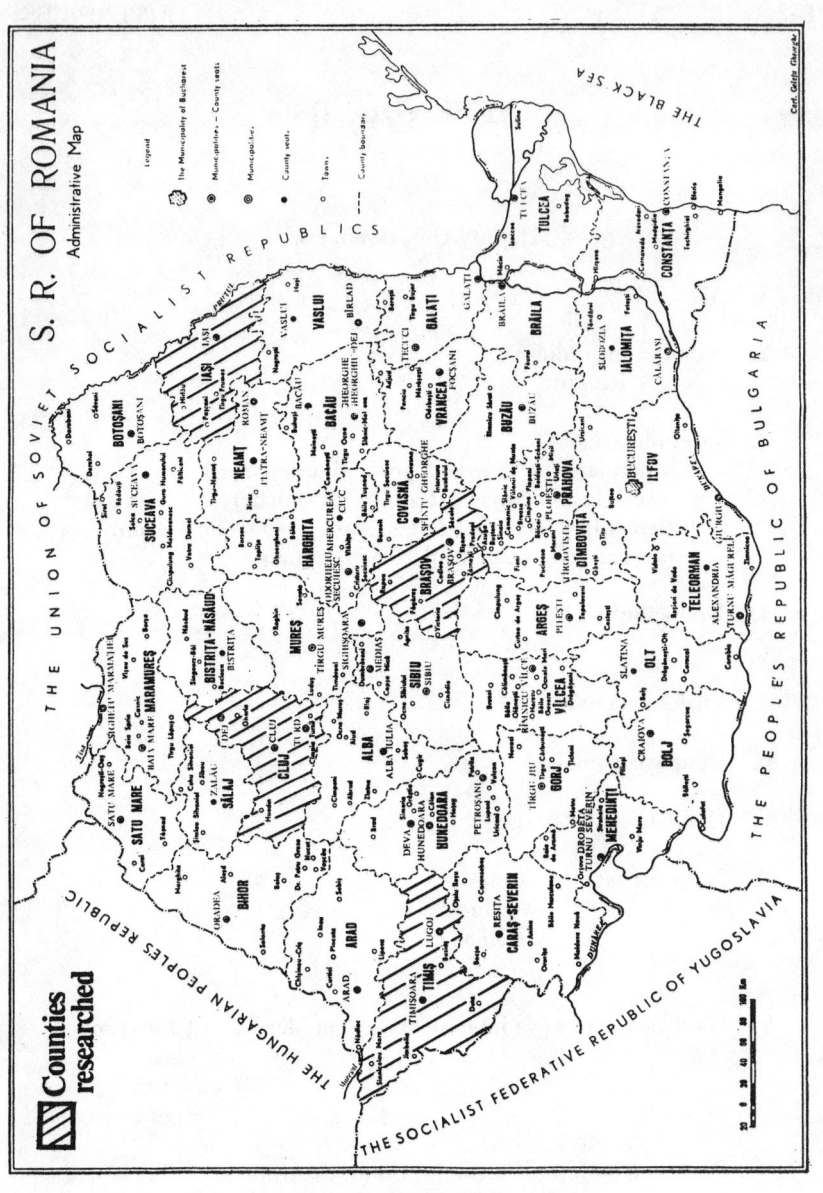

MAP OF RESEARCH AREAS

APPENDIX A

152   APPENDICES

APPENDIX B

Deputy Questionnaire

1. Virsta:

2. Sexul: masculin
             feminin

3. Ce studii aveți?
   superioare (inclusiv pedagogic și subingineri)
   medii (licee tehnice și școli professionale)
   elementare (școli primare și școli generale de 7-8 ani)
   fara școala și școli primare neterminate

4. Domiciliul: Oraș
                 Comuna

5. Profesia da baza:

6. Ocupația actuala:

7. Ocupația anteriora:

8. Naționalitatea: Româna
                      Maghiara
                      Germana
                      De alte Naționalitați

9. Cînd a început sa va intereseze viața publica?   Adolescent
                                                     Tinar
                                                     Matur
                                                     Batrîn

10. Sunteți membru al Partidului Comunist Român?   Da
                                                    Nu

11. Ce alte activitați ați desfașurat în viața publica înaintea alegerii
    ca deputat?

Appendices   153

12. Ce functie îndepliniți acum în sistemul consiliului popular?
    președinte, vice-președinte sau secretar al unei comisii
        permanente
    membru în comitetul executiv
    președinte, vice-președinte sau secretar al comitetul executive
    funcționar în aparatul consiliului popular
    lucrator în unitațile subordonate consiliului popular
    altele

13. Credeți ca activitatea și raspunderea în servicile publice va fi pe
    viitor privind problema individual:
        mai mare decît în prezent
        mai mica decît în present
        aceeaș

14. Sunteți mumbru al uneia din organizațiile mai jos amintite?
        Uniune
        Sindicat
        Societate culturala
        Organizație sportiva
        Organizație artistica
        Organizație religioasa
        Organizație voluntara de ajutor reciproc
        Club de ocupație distractiva
        Club de tineri
        Club de pionieri
        Altele   care?

15. Cum ați participat la vreuna sau la mai multe din organizațiile
    de mai sus?
        permanent
        din cînd în cînd
        niciodata

16. Care ar fi cele mai importante probleme de rezolvat ale Consiliilor
    Populare Județene in viitor (1-3) ani?

17. Care este cea mai importanta problema a Consiliului Popular
    Județean (municipal, comunal) in viitor dupa parerea Dv.?

18. Pe ce cai s-ar putea perfectiona activitatea consiliului popular?
        Reducerea numarului de deputați
        Mai buna pregatire a sesiunii

154   APPENDICES

       Prelungirea duratei sesiunii
       Creşterea numarului de deputaţi
       O mai buna activitate a comisiilor permanente
       Altele   Care?

19. Care este cea mai importanta activitate pe care Consiliul Popular o desfaşoara pentru public?

20. Exista organizaţiile cu caracter nepolitic care influenţeaza viaţa publica a judeţului (oraşului, etc.) dumneavoastra?
       Da   Daca da, cum?
       Nu

21. Care sunt metodele, ori mijloacele Consiliilor Populare ori ale altor instituţii guvernamentale locale, intrebuinţate, pentru a atrage şi cointeresa cetaţenii în viaţa publica?

22. Care este modalitatea de a deveni deputat al Consiliilor Populare?

23. Dezvoltarea sociala şi economica a Republicii Socialiste Romania d din ultimele decade a facut ca activitatea Consiliilor Populare sa fie:
       importante şi complexa
       la fel ca în anii precedenţi
       simplificata

24. Ce atribuţii noi are Consiliuli Popular în prezent, pe care nu le-a avut în trecut?

25. Care ar trebui sa fie problemele cele mai mult dezbatute de Consiliul Popular local?
       probleme de industrie
       probleme de agricultura
       comerţ
       învaţamînt şi cultura
       probleme de sanatate
       probleme gospodareşti
       alte probleme, care?
       nu ştiu

26. Ce caracter au problemele ridicate de cetaţeni?
       propuneri cu caracter general sau obştesc
       propuneri cu caracter personal
       reclamaţii şi sesizari cu caracter general sau obştesc
       reclamaţii şi sesizari cu caracter personal
       altele   care?

APPENDIX C

THE DATA BASE

Table C_1 indicates the distribution of deputy interviews conducted for this study. The number of deputies interviewed varied from county to county due to circumstances (such as lack of cooperation, remoteness of communes, weather, etc.) that imposed upon the sample a bias towards urban areas. The extent of this sampling error is presented in Figure I. When considering results of interviews, this lack of a proportionate sample necessitated weighting the data, which will be explained below.

Aside from the difficulty indicated above, a comparison between deputies interviewed and the total population of deputies in three of the four counties where research was conducted indicates no *serious* bias —that is, the sample does not greatly misrepresent the composition of people's councils in these locations. (In Timiş County, less cooperation was received, and the sample is not only smaller but more skewed than the other counties toward urban localities. It is reasonsable to assume, then, that its biases are more pronounced.) Table C_2, for example, exhibits for Cluj, Braşov, and Iaşi counties the percentages of deputies in the sample with certain backgrounds compared to percentages of the deputy population with the same characteristics. There are, to be sure, the inevitable sampling errors that any sample drawn from a larger group entails. These necessitated making only *tentative inferences* from sample to population.

As Table C_2 demonstrates, the samples from three of the four counties are skewed in two principal directions *vis-a-vis* the population of deputies. First, there is an over-representation of "intellectual" and "other" occupational categories concomitant with an underrepresentation of peasants. Second, an over-representation of deputies over fifty years of age corresponds to an underrepresentation of those under thirty-five years old.

Both of these biases have readily understandable origins, and are not necessarily so large that the accuracy of the sample can be doubted on the

TABLE C₁
DEPUTY INTERVIEWS: DISTRIBUTION OF SAMPLE BY TYPE OF LOCATION

Location		Timiș	Cluj	Brașov	Iași	Total
County	N =	3	12	20	19	54
	% of County Total =	8.1	25.5	40	29.7	27.3
Town/City (oraș/municipiu)	N =	23	17	22	20	82
	% of County Total =	62.2	36.2	44	31.3	41.4
Commune (comuna)	N =	11	18	8	25	62
	% of County Total =	29.7	38.3	16	39.1	31.3
Totals	N =	37	47	50	64	198
	% of County Total =	100	100	100	100	100

FIGURE I

Percentage of Sample by Type of Location vs.
Percentage in Actual Deputy Population

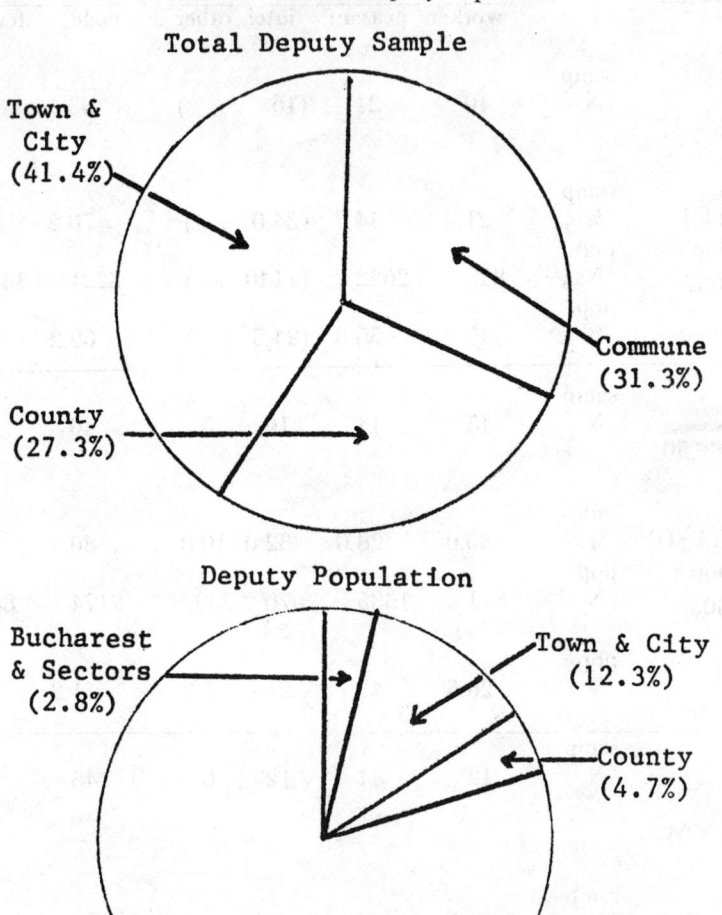

158   APPENDICES

TABLE C[2]

Comparison of Sample with Actual Population of Deputies[a]

County		Base Occupation [b]				Sex	
		worker	peasant	intel.	other	male	female
Ns = 47	samp N	10	21	(16	)	33	14
CLUJ	samp %	21.3	44.7	(34.0	)	70.2	29.8
Npop = 1657	pop N	895	2622	(1140	)	3221	1436
	pop %	19.2	56.3	(24.5	)	69.2	30.8
Ns = 50	samp N	15	14	16	5	40	10
BRAȘOV	samp %	30.0	28.0	32.0	10.0	80	20
Npop = 3055	pop N	811	1335	670	239	2174	881
	pop %	26.5	43.7	21.9	7.8	71.2	28.8
Ns = 64	samp N	12	34	12	6	45	19
IAȘI	samp %	18.8	53.1	18.8	9.4	70.3	29.7
Npop = 5286	pop N	814	3436	676	360	3658	1628
	pop %	15.4	65.0	12.8	6.8	69.2	30.8

Appendices 159

TABLE C 2 (Continued)

County		Age			Nationality		
		Under 35	35-50	Over 50	Rom.	Hung.	Other
CLUJ	samp N	10	27	10	39	8	–
	samp %	21.3	57.4	21.3	83.0	17.0	–
	pop N	1356	2421	879	3777	867	12
	pop %	29.1	52.0	18.9	81.1	18.6	0.3
BRAȘOV	samp N	10	27	13	36	8	Germ 6
	samp %	20.0	54.0	26.0	72.0	16.0	Germ 12.0
	pop N	743	1740	572	2271	377	Germ 407
	pop %	24.3	57.0	18.7	74.3	12.3	Germ 13.3
IAȘI	samp N	14	35	15	63	–	1
	samp %	21.9	54.7	23.4	98.4	–	1.5
	pop N	1536	2776	974	5268	–	18
	pop %	29.1	52.5	18.4	99.5	–	0.5

a   Based on county-wide data from 1969 elections; Timiș figures unavailable.

b   Occupational categories: "workers" include laborers, craftsmen, technicians; "peasants" includes collectivized and non-collectivized; "intellectual" includes engineers, economists, professors, teachers, doctors, scientists, artists, etc.; "other" includes police, housewives, party cadre, mass organization workers, state administrators, etc.

160   APPENDICES

whole. The "intellectual" and "other" occupational categories are clearly
related to the disproportionate presence of urban or municipal deputies
in the sample (since those occupations are more present in cities), which
is in turn due to research circumstances suggested earlier. Standardization
of the sample as to deputies' location by weighting the communal and
county samples also reduced the influence of such an occupational bias.

That the sample tends to be older than the population of deputies
results from the greater availability of professional people and pensioners.
In the first place, directors, managers, and foremen (who tend to be
older than the people whom they oversee) were able to leave their jobs
much more freely than production-line workers, sales clerks, etc., for
interviews. Moreover, pensioners were eager to be interviewed, and their
over-representation raised the sample's overall age composition slightly.
Thus, despite generally cooperative efforts of local officials to obtain a
representative sample for me, these biases persisted.

Sampling problems thus far indicated necessarily affect one's confidence in the extent to which the sample is representative of the deputy
population in any one of the research counties. A confidence level will
obviously be adversely affected by an unavoidably small sample, and
biases toward certain occupational categories, older age groups and urban
localities. Had I been able to obtain a larger sample, I would not have
hesitated to eliminate an appropriate proportion of interviews from
over-represented categories of essential background characteristics. Unable to interview more deputies alone, however, I have chosen to use
almost the entire sample (save for a few interviews that were not at all
substantive), recognizing the interpretive difficulties this poses.

Any test of a sample relative to the population from which it was
drawn has the objective of finding whether or not a significant difference exists between characteristics of the sample and characteristics of
the population; i.e., to test the "goodness-of-fit." Chi-square (x^2) is the
most commonly used statistic for this purpose.

An example can better illustrate this test. Occupational backgrounds
of the sample and actual deputy population, for instance, can be seen
to vary in Table C_2 for Cluj County. One should know the degree to
which that difference would lead us to doubt any inferences made from
the responses of such a sampling of deputies. A calculation of x^2 for that
section of Table C_2 yields 2.95 which, when there are 2 degree of freedom

Appendices

(df = 2), is significant at .23. One cannot, therefore, reject the null hypothesis, which means that tentative assumptions can be made about the sample's accuracy.

With that level of significance, however, one is led to some healthy skepticims about any generalizations to be made—a warning already cited. Yet, x^2 is certainly not equal to or greater than what is needed for P = .05 (at df = 2), which social scientists conventionally accept in statistical tests. There is no cause, then, to reject generalizations made from the sample with any confidence. On the other hand, inferences must be made with the knowledge that the sample is very small, prohibiting the levels of confidence for which one might hope.

Most of the other sections of Table C2 have chi squares which point to *greater* assurance that the sample is not seriously biased. One can be a bit more confident in the case of the Cluj sample's age distribution, for example, with an x^2 that is significant at P = .50. Differences between the samples' and population's sex and nationality characteristics are smaller yet. X^2 calculations suggest that the differences that do exist would give one almost no reason to reject generalizations made from the deputies' responses during interviews (i.e., chi squares are significant only at higher probabilities). (For a complete table of chi-square scores and corresponding levels of significance based on Table C2, see Table C3).

Other influences, of course, could affect the validity of this book's data. A possible tendency for the respondents to answer my questions in a way they thought would be "appropriate" to the situation, as opposed to what they "truly believed," is a potentiality that must be taken into account. Generally, there is little a researcher can do to assure that subjects are being totally "open." One can, however, broadly distinguish between "objective" and "subjective" comments, and even design questions to obtain answers of both types.

Moreover, as was the case with questions I used, a degree of "overlap" can be planned among questions such that one answer will tend to be supported or refuted by another. These "checks" on potentially invalid responses are rather effective when combined. If my subjective assessments and their response inconsistencies confirmed one another, the interview was not considered as part of the data. Because of my small sample, I was reluctant to void an interview unless all indications were that the session had produced responses without substance—i.e., that were irrelevant for my purposes.

TABLE C 3

SUMMATION OF CHI SQUARE ("GOODNESS-OF-FIT") SCORES AND CORRESPONDING LEVELS OF SIGNIFICANCE

	Base Occupation	Sex	CLUJ Age	Nationality
	X^2 Signif. at:	X^2 Signif. at:	X^2 Signif. at:	X^2 Signif. at:
	2.95 df = 2, P = .23	.024 df = 1, P = .85	1.39 df = 2, P = .50	.20 df = 2, P = .90
BRAȘOV	5.57 df = 3, P = .13	1.88 df = 1, P = .17	1.84 df = 2, P = .60	.63 df = 2, P = .73
IAȘI	4.19 df = 3, P = .24	.037 df = 1, P = .83	2.04 df = 2, P = .36	2.82 df = 2, .20 < P < .30

APPENDICES

Appendices

163

Another bias to which a sample of deputies is subject might be an over-representation of certain functions in the people's council apparatus—that is, more executive committee members than there would have been in a sample exactly proportionate to the deputy population. A question was inserted mid-way in the questionnaire to ascertain the degree of such a bias. Responses suggest that, for the most part, samples drawn from Cluj, Brașov and Iași counties were not biased towards executive committee members; of the Cluj sample 10.6% is from the executive committee, while 14.0% of the Brașov respondents and 14.1% in Iași are from that organ of local government. These figures are approximately what one might expect if the sample were to represent the deputy population. Of 37 Timiș deputies, however, 8 (or almost 22%) were executive committee members, indicating another cause to be doubtful of any generalizations made from that sample.

The unavoidable bias towards urban deputies (leading to further, but less serious, occupational and age biases) necessitated weighting the data such that responses would be distributed proportionately according to locations as in the actual deputy population. The method used to weight the data here was, quite simply, to obtain a "correction factor" for each level of each county. This was done by dividing the percentage of the deputy population at each level in each county by the percentage of the sample from the same level in each county. The resulting correction factors (or "weights") for all counties is indicated in Table C4. These "weights" were utilized in the calculation of all percentage tables in Chapter IV.

TABLE C 4

CORRECTION FACTORS FOR LOCATION

County	Level	% Pop. Ratio / % in Sample	Correction Factor
Timiş	Town-City	$\frac{13.0}{62.2}$	.209
Timiş	County	$\frac{4.4}{8.1}$	.543
Timiş	Commune	$\frac{82.6}{29.7}$	2.78
Cluj	Town-City	$\frac{14.3}{36.2}$	.395
Cluj	County	$\frac{4.5}{25.5}$	.176
Cluj	Commune	$\frac{81.2}{38.3}$	2.12
Braşov	Town-City	$\frac{22.9}{44}$	.520
Braşov	County	$\frac{6.6}{40}$	.165
Braşov	Commune	$\frac{70.5}{16}$	4.406
Iaşi	Town-City	$\frac{7.5}{31.25}$	.240
Iaşi	County	$\frac{4.2}{29.7}$	.141
Iaşi	Commune	$\frac{88.3}{39.06}$	2.26

FOOTNOTES

1. As a "comparative" study, it follows that similarities and differences among units considered will be used to make generalizable, albeit tentative, conclusions.

2. James Coleman, *Crises and Sequences in Political Development* (Princeton: Princeton University Press, 1971), pp. 78-79.

3. Richard P. Applebaum, *Theories of Social Change* (Chicago: Markham, 1970), pp. 15-59.

4. Ralf Dahrendorf, *Class and Class Conflict in Industrial Society* (Stanford: Stanford University Press, 1959), pp. 158-59.

5. Samuel P. Huntington, *Political Order in Changing Societies* (New Haven: Yale University Press, 1968), p. 5.

6. Ronald D. Brunner and Garry D. Brewer, *Organized Complexity* (New York: Free Press, 1971), pp. 1-2.

7. David E. Apter, *Politics of Modernization* (Chicago: University of Chicago Press, 1965), p. 393.

8. Ibid., p. 421.

9. John H. Kautsky, *The Political Consequences of Modernization* (New York: John Wiley & Sons, 1972), p. 9.

10. Ibid., p. 172.

11. Lucian Pye, *Aspects of Political Development* (Boston: Little, Brown & Co., 1966), pp. 64-65.

12. Cyril E. Black, *The Dynamics of Modernization* (New York: Harper & Row, 1966), p. 27.

13. Robert T. Holt and John E. Turner, *The Political Basis of Economic Development* (Princeton: D.Van Nostrand, 1966), p. 329.

14. Joseph LaPalombara, "Parsimony and Empiricism in Comparative Politics: An Anti-Scholastic View," in *The Methodology of Comparative*

Comparative Research, ed. Robert T. Holt and John E. Turner (New York: Free Press, 1970), p. 148.

15. Norman N. Nie, G. Bingham Powell, and Kenneth Prewitt, "Social Structure and Political Participation: Developmental Relationships," *The American Political Science Review*, LXIII, No. 2 (June 1969), 370.

16. James A. Bill and Robert L. Hardgrave, *Comparative Politics: The Quest for Theory* (Columbus, Ohio, Charles E. Merrill, 1973), p. 79.

17. Richard Lowenthal, "Development vs. Utopia in Communist Policy," in *Change in Communist Systems*, ed. Chalmers Johnson (Stanford: Stanford University Press, 1970), p. 53.

18. Peter C. Ludz, *The Changing Party Elite in East Germany* (Cambridge: The MIT Press, 1972), p. 1. (Emphasis added.).

19. Ibid., footnote no. 1, p. 1.

20. Ibid., pp. 1-4.

21. Dennis Pirages, "Socioeconomic Development and Political Access in the Communist Party-States," in *Communist Party-States*, ed. Jan F. Triska (Indianapolis: Bobbs-Merrill Co., 1969), pp. 249-81.

22. Ibid., p. 255.

23. Jan F. Triska and Paul M. Johnson, "Political Development and Political Change," in Carmelo Mesa-Lago and Carl Beck, eds., *Comparative Socialist Systems* (Pittsburgh: UCIS, 1975), p. 283.

24. A. Eckstein, "Economic Development and Political Change in Communist Systems," in *World Politics* 22 (July 1970), p. 475.

25. Ibid., p. 492.

26. See, for example, John Kautsky, *Communism and Political Development* (New York: John Wiley & Sons, 1968), who sees that communist movements can be most productively viewed as modernizing movements; Keith Rush, "The Reforms: A Balance Sheet," *Problems of Communism* (July-August 1967), where it is reported that the Soviet sub-national councils of ministers face growing problems arising from development; or Alf Edeen, "The Administrative Intelligentsia," *Survey*, No. 65 (October 1967), 61-74, who deals with the increasing diversity and complexity of Soviet society due to development and modernization, and the results of those changes on administration.

27. *Fundamentals of Marxism-Leninism* (Moscow, 1961), pp. 94-95, quoted in David Lane, *Politics and Society in the USSR* (New York: Random House, 1971), p. 4.

Notes   167

28. L.G. Churchward, "Soviet Local Government Today," *Soviet Studies*, XVII, No. 4 (April 1966), 431-52. (Emphasis added.)

29. *World Bank Atlas, 1972* (Washington, D.C.: International Bank for Reconstruction and Development, 1972).

30. Vasile Rausser, "Romania's Economic Relations with the Developing Countries," *Revue Roumaine des Sciences Sociales: Serie de Sciences Economiques*, Tome 16, No. 2 (1972), 195.

31. Nicolae Ceauşescu, *Raport la Conferinţa Naţtionala a Partidului Comunist Român*, Iulie 1972 (Bucureşti: Editura Politica, 1972), p. 98.

32. "Declaraţie cu privire la posiţia Partidului Muncitoresc Român în Problemele mişcarii Comuniste şi Muncitoreşti internaţionale, adoptata de Plenara largita a C.C. al P.M.R. din Aprilie, 1964" (Bucureşti: Editura Politica, 1964).

33. Nicolae Ceauşescu, *Romania pe drumul construirii societaţii socialiste multilateral dezvoltate*, Vols. I-VIII, 1969-73 (Bucureşti: Editura Politica, 1969-73).

34. See the factors listed by Claude E. Welch, Jr., ed. *Political Modernization* (Belmont, California: Wadsworth, 1967), pp. 2-6.

35. William Bascom, for instance, has pointed this out in his article, "Urbanization Among the Yoruba," *The American Journal of Sociology*, Vol. 60, 1955, 446-54.

36. Daniel Lerner, "Comparative Analysis of Process of Modernization," in *Comparative Research Across Cultures and Nations*, ed. Stein Rokkan (The Hague: Mouton, 1968), p. 82; Marion J. Levy, *Modernization and the Structure of Societies* (Princeton: Princeton University Press, 1966), p. 11; most blatantly, W.E. Moore in *Social Change* (Englewood Cliffs, N.J.: Prentice-Hall, 1963), p. 93.

37. Adapted from U.S. Congress, 91st, 2nd Session, Joint Economic Committee, *Economic Developments in Countries of Eastern Europe* (Washington, D.C.: GPO, 1970).

38. Alan A. Brown and Paul Marer, "Foreign Trade in the East European Reforms," in *Plan and Market*, ed. M. Bornstein (New Haven: Yale University Press, 1973), pp. 156-59 passim.

39. Hubert M. Blalock, *Social Statistics* (New York: McGraw-Hill, 1960), p. 13.

40. Ibid., p. 14.

168   NOTES

41. The sequence of calculations is taken from Sidney Siegel, *Non-parametric Statistics* (New York: McGraw-Hill, 1956), pp. 229-32.

42. Ibid., p. 286, Appendix Table R.

43. Ibid., p. 237.

44. Zbigniew Brzezinski, *The Soviet Bloc* (Cambridge: Harvard University Press, 1969), p. 77.

45. For example in Ghiţa Ionescu, *Communism in Rumania, 1944-1962* (London, 1964), pp. 71ff and Stephen Fischer-Galaţi, *The New Rumania* (Cambridge, Mass.: MIT Press, 1967), pp. 17ff.

46. Fischer-Galaţi, op. cit., p. 40.

47. Ion Vîntu et al., *Sfaturile Populare: Organe Locale ale Puterii de Stat în RPR* (Bucureşti: Editura Academiei Republicii Populare Romîne, 1964), p. 55.

48. Ibid., pp. 49-52.

49. See Paul Lendvai, *Eagles in Cobwebs: Nationalism and Communism in the Balkans* (Garden City, N.Y.: Anchor Books, 1969); others like Ghiţa Ionescu refer to a renewed patriotism tempered by realism, *Communism in Rumania*, op. cit., p. 348; other interpretations suggest a "nationalization of communism" has taken place, as does Gabriel Fischer in *The Communist States in Disarray*, ed. Adam Bromke and Teresa Rakowska-Harmstone (Minneapolis: University of Minnesota Press, 1972). The essence of these various ideas, I think, remains that a renewed nationalism is again evident in Romania.

50. Ion Vîntu, "Romania," in *Central Services to Local Authorities in Selected Eastern European Countries and the USSR* (New York: The United Nations, 1970), p. 145.

51. Nicolae Ceauşescu, *Raport la Conferinţa Naţionala a Partidului Comunist Român, Decembrie, 1967* (Bucureşti: Editura Politica, 1967), p. 16.

52. Yugoslavia also claimed that title, but to the rest of the Communist Europe, that has been a heretical claim.

53. The most complete treatment of these periodic administrative changes is *Ion Vîntu et al., Sfaturile Populare*, op. cit., pp. 37-66, in Chapter I, entitled "Formarea şi Dezvoltarea Organelor Locale ale Puterii de Stat în Republica Populara Româna."

54. H. Gordon Skilling, *The Governments of Communist East Europe* (New York: Crowell, 1966), p. 54.

Notes 169

55. Vîntu, *Central Services to Local Authority*, op. cit., p. 149. See also similar observations regarding the Soviet Union in Alfred E. Meyer, *The Soviet Political System* (New York: Random House, 1965), p. 200.

56. Oral comments made to the author, July 2, 1973, Bucharest. Such a cynicism does not mean that academic circles or the educated population would care not at all if people's councils or the Grand National Assembly did not exist. Indeed, the continued presence of quasi-representative bodies *is* regarded to be important by academicians insofar as these organs exist, occasionally serving to focus on national problems or operating as channels of citizen-regime communication.

57. Ghita Ionescu, *The Politics of the European Communist States* (New York: Praeger, 1967), p. 39.

58. Ion Vîntu, *Sfaturile Populare*, op. cit., "Introducere," p. 17.

59. *The Constitution of the Socialist Republic of Romania*, "Chapter V: The Local Bodies of State Power and the Local Bodies of State Administration, Article 79" (Bucharest: Meridiane, 1969), p. 31.

60. The size of people's councils was reduced by the December 1974 Election Law revision to this Law. The quoted ranges, however, are accurate for the period when this research was conducted; see *Lege de Organizare și Funcționare a Consiliilor Populare* (București: Editura Politica, 1968), pp. 12-13.

61. These ranges are simple means of the total number of deputies at each level, divided by the number of units at that level; data obtained from *Buletinul Oficial al Republicii Socialiste România*, Anul V, Nr. 50 (5 Marție, 1969), p. 2.

62. *Lege de Organizare și funcționare a Consiliilor Populare*, op. cit., "Chapter IV, Article 28," pp. 16-17.

63. Ibid., "Chapter VI, Article 48," p. 29.

64. Constitution, op. cit., "Article 3" and "Article 26," respectively.

65. Nicolae Ceaușescu, *Raport... Decembrie*, 1967, op. cit., pp. 117-18.

66. Ibid., p. 118.

67. Ion Vîntu, M. Anghene, and Mirceau Straoanu, *Organele Administrației de Stat în Republica Socialistă România* (București: Editura Academiei Republicii Socialiste Romania, 1971), p. 223.

68. Gheorghe Bobocea, "Organizarea administrative-teritoriala—factor organizator al vieții social-economice," *Lupta de Clasa*, 1967, Nr. 11;

170   NOTES

also Petre Blajovic, "Cerințe noi în Organizarea Teritoriala și Sistematizarea Rurala," *Probleme Economice*, 1967, Nr. 11, pp. 3-18.

69. Nicolae Ceaușescu, *Raport. . . Iulie 1972*, op. cit., p. 72.

70. Leonard Schapiro, *The Communist Party of the Soviet Union* (New York: Vintage 1971), p. 448; also *The CPSU in Resolutions*, 7th ed. (Moscow, 1953), Part I, p. 467 as quoted in *The Communist Party Aparatus*, Abdurakhman Avtorkhanov (Cleveland: Meridian, 1968), p. 119.

71. Avtorkhanov, op. cit., p. 5.

72. V.I. Lenin, *On Party Construction* (Moscow: 1956), p. 349, cited in ibid., p. 6.

73. Nicolae Ceaușescu, *Raport. . . Iulie 1972*, op. cit., p. 76.

74. Ion Vîntu et al., *Organele Locale ale Administrației de Stat*, op. cit., pp. 309-10; see also *Hotarirea Consiliului de Miniștri*, Nr. 1,096 of 1970.

75. Chalmers Johnson, "Comparing Communist Nations," in *Change in Communist Systems*, ed. Chalmers Johnson, op. cit., p. 8.

76. *Lege de Organizare și Funcționare a Consiliilor Populare*, op. cit., "Chapter VI, Section 1."

77. Ion Vîntu, "Centralisme et autonomie," *Res Publica*, Vol. XIII (1971), No. 5, pp. 757-58.

78. "Nomenklatura" is a Russian term variously defined in Western literature. Most recently, Robert J. Osborn has written that nomenklatura can "perhaps best" be "translated as 'patronage'," in *The Evolution of Soviet Politics* (Homeward, Ill.: Dorsey Press, 1974), p. 283; while Darrell P. Hammer has argued that the phrase "power of appointment" is the best translation, in *U.S.S.R.: The Politics of Oligarchy* (Hinsdale, Ill.: The Dryden Press, 1974), p. 197.

79. Ghița Ionescu, *Communism in Rumania*, op. cit., p. 167, and *Politics of the European Communist States*, op. cit., p. 55.

80. Ionescu, *Politics of the European Communist States*, op. cit., p. 63.

81. Chalmers Johnson, "Comparing Communist Nations," in op. cit., p. 14.

82. Ibid., (Emphases added.)

83. One should again recall that these numbers were reduced in elections of March 9, 1975 when only 51,441 deputies were elected nationwide, only about one-third the previous number. The erstwhile "democratic

Notes 171

base" of the regime is, then, being narrowed. These data are from *Buletinul Oficial al Republicii Socialiste Romania*, Partea aII-a, Nr. 40 (1969), p. 172.

84. Gabriel Almond, ed., *Comparative Politics Today: A World View* (Boston: Little, Brown and Co., 1974), p. 209.

85. *Front De L'Unite Socialiste: Documents Constitutifs* (București: Editions Meridiane, 1972), passim.

86. See the list of organizations included in the S.U.F. in *Scînteia Tineretului* (București: December 20, 1968), p. 1.

87. L.W. Milbrath, *Political Participation* (Chicago: Rand-McNally, 1965), pp. 13ff.

88. S. Tarrow, "The Urban-Renewal Cleavage in Political Involvement," *The American Political Science Review*, 65 (June 1971), 341-57.

89. These qualities of participation in a democratic political system are mentioned by Alexander J. Groth in *Comparative Politics: A Distributive Approach* (New York: MacMillan, 1971), p. 28.

90. Nie, Powell, and Prewitt, op. cit.

91. See Frederic J. Fleron, "Co-optation as a Mechanism of Adaptation to Change: The Soviet Political Leadership System," *Polity*, II (1969), 176-201.

92. Fischer-Galați, *The New Rumania*, op. cit., p. 39.

93. Question Twelve was utilized earlier in this chapter as part of a consideration of the sample's validity. Question Thirteen, which asked: "Do you think your activities in public life will increase, decrease or remain the same in the future?", did not produce differentiated responses; over 90% of all deputies interviewed stated that they expected their involvement to increase.

94. Samuel P. Huntington, op. cit., pp. 33-35, especially Huntington's citation of Deutsch, p. 33.

95. Ibid., p. 50, for example.

96. Oral communication, October, 1973.

97. See, for example, the communique issued by the Executive Committee of the Central Committee of the Romanian Communist Party after its February 5, 1974 meeting in *Romania: Documents-Events*, Vol. 4, No. 5 (January 1974).

98. Oral communications, both from September, 1973.

99. Oral communications, October, 1973.

172 NOTES

100. Oral communication, August, 1973.

101. Oral communication, October, 1973.

102. Oral communication, August, 1973.

103. Oral communication, September, 1973.

104. Clientele systems have been increasingly the subject of social science investigation; see, for example, John D. Powell, "Peasant Society and the Clientelist Politics," *American Political Science Review*, 64; 411-24 (June 1970); Alex Weingrod, "Patrons, Patronage and Political Parties," *Comparative Studies in Society and History*, Vol. 10, 376-400 (July 1969); and James C. Scott, "Corruption, Machine Politics, and Political Change," *American Political Science Review*, 62: 1142-58 (December 1969). Most of such studies, and other in anthropological literature, agree that a clientele system involves "an exchange of noncomparable goods and services between actors of unequal socio-economic ranks" (Powell's phrase) that manifests itself in political behavior "such as nepotism, personalism, or favoritism . . . " (again Powell's statement). This, of course, is not *precisely* my meaning here, but insofar as Romania shares with other developing/modernizing states the penetration of an older peasant society into present-day culture, comparisons can be made.

105. "Gospodar" is a Romanian noun (derived from "gospodarea") which has no English equivalent but can be approximated by the phrase "household manager"; when applied in a civic sense, "gospodarea" becomes "public service and maintenance."

106. Oral communication, October, 1973.

107. From statistics provided to the author by officials of the Cluj Municipal People's Council.

108. *Anuarul Statistic*, op. cit.; previously cited in Table IV.

109. *Law No. 28 of 1966 Regulating the Election of Deputies to the Grand National Assembly and the People's Councils* (Bucharest: Meridiane Publishing House, 1969), Article 38.

110. The genuine "surprise" of which I speak was revealed to me in many interviews with deputies who were outside both the local political elite and an important circle of deputies.

111. This opinion was expressed to the author, in varying forms, on several occasions, but most strongly in an oral communication, July 1973, with officials of the Timişoara people's council.

112. Gabriel Almond has written, for instance, that within a modern

Notes 173

industrial-democratic nation there is usually a group of ten percent of the adult population who are "hardly aware of government and politics at all. They may be illiterate, *rural people living in remote areas,* or older women, unresponsive to female suffrage, who are almost entirely involved in their families and communities. We call these people *parochials.*" (First emphasis added.) "Introduction," in *Comparative Politics Today* (Boston: Little, Brown and Co., 1974), p. 50.

113. William A. Welsh, "Toward a Multiple-Strategy Approach to Research on Comparative Communist Political Elites: Empirical and Qualitative Problems," in *Communist Studies and the Social Sciences: Essays on Methodology and Empirical Theory,* ed. Frederic J. Fleron, Jr. (Chicago, Rand McNally, 1969), pp. 318-56.

114. See, for instance, Zbigniew K. Brzezinski, *The Permanent Purge: Politics in Soviet Political Succession in the USSR* (New York: Columbia University Press, 1965).

115. William A. Welsh, "Introduction," in *Comparative Communist Political Leadership* ed. Carl Beck, et al. (New York: David McKay, 1973), pp. 3-4.

116. Ibid., p. 120.

117. Ibid., p. 61.

118. *Lege. . . , 1968, op. cit., p. 29.*

119. Ibid.

120. Nicolae Ceaușescu, in *Viitorul Social,* Septembrie, 1972, p. 7.

121. This is a paraphrase of a statement made to me in an oral communication, July 1973, by a current political elite at the local level; what that person said, however, is no different than less explicit information with which most students of communist regimes are familiar.

122. Oral communication, July 1973.

123. Oral communication, August, 1973.

124. Biographical information provided to the author through interviews, August, 1973.

125. Nicolae Ceaușescu,in *Viitorul Social,* op. cit., p. 8.

126. I was informed of this law in an oral communication, October, 1973.

127. See, for example, the text written for internal consumption: *Organizaţiile obşteşti în sistemul organizarii politice din Republica Socialista România* (Bucureşti: Editura Academiei Republicii Socialiste România, 1973), p. 35.

174   NOTES

128. J. Demeter, E. Eisenburger, and V. Lipatti, *Romania and the National Question* (Bucharest: Meridiane, 1972), p. 58.

129. Abdurakhman Avtorkhanov, op. cit., p. 59.

130. Nicolae Ceauşescu, "Speech at the Working Meeting of the Party Active from the Sphere of Ideology and Political and Cultural-Educational Activity," July 9, 1971.

131. Ibid., p. 7.

132. See, for instance, *Scînteia*, Saturday, November 17, 1973, where he again noted the need for better prepared cadres—real cadres, not just names on lists, he states—to remedy many problems that he cites in that major speech.

133. Fischer in *Communist States in Disarray*, op. cit., p. 178.

134. Abdurakhman Avtorkhanov, op. cit., p. 67.

135. Ibid., p. 62, from Stalin's February, 1931 Speech to a congress of factory workers in J.V. Stalin, *Problems of Leninism* (Moscow, 1947), p. 326.

136. Richard Cornell, ed., *The Soviet Political System: A Book of Readings* (Englewood Cliffs, N.J.: Prentice-Hall, 1970), p. 135.

137. Oral communication, July, 1973.

138. Oral communication, July, 1973.

139. Oral communication, July, 1973.

140. Oral communication, July, 1973.

141. Oral communication, July, 1973.

142. Oral communication, August, 1973.

143. Oral communication, September, 1973.

144. Oral communication, September, 1973.

145. Oral communication, September, 1973.

146. Oral communication, September, 1973.

147. Oral communication, October, 1973.

148. Oral communication, October, 1973.

149. Oral communication, October, 1973.

150. Oral communication, October, 1973.

151. Oral communication, October, 1973.

152. Oral communication, October, 1973.

153. Lucian W. Pye, "Identity and the Political Culture," in *Crises and Sequences in Political Development*, op. cit., p. 129.

154. Gabriel Fischer, op. cit., p. 174.

Notes 175

155. Oral communication, October, 1973.

156. Oral communication, October, 1973.

157. Oral communication, October, 1973.

158. Oral communication, July, 1973.

159. This is a paraphrase of how Darrell P. Hammer describes Lenin's leadership vis-a-vis Stalin's autocracy, op. cit., p. 2.

160. Concerning the rise of "consumerism" in Eastern Europe, see J.F. Brown, "Soviet Polity in Eastern Europe and the Impact of Detente," in *Eastern European Perspectives on European Security and Cooperation*, ed. R.R. King and R.W. Dean (New York: Praeger, 1974).

161. Oral communication, October, 1973.

162. Oral communication, October, 1973.

163. Oral communication, October, 1973.

164. Oral communication, October, 1973.

165. Oral communication, July, 1973.

166. Oral communication, September, 1973.

167. L.F. Anderson, M.W. Watts, Jr., and A.R. Wilcox, *Legislative Roll-Call Analysis* (Evanston, Ill.: Northwestern University Press, 1966), pp. 34-35.

168. Morton Gorden, *Comparative Political Systems: Managing Conflict* (New York: MacMillan, 1972), p. 117.

169. Ibid., pp. 117-18.

170. James A. Bill and Robert L. Hardgrave, op. cit., pp. 75-76.

171. Charles W. Anderson, Fred R. von der Mehden, and Crawford Young, *Issues of Political Development* (Englewood Cliffs, N.J.: Prentice-Hall, 1974), pp. 231-32.

172. Chalmers Johnson, "Comparing Communist Nations," in Chalmers Johnson, op. cit., p. 15.

BIBLIOGRAPHY

BOOKS

Academiei Republicii Socialiste România. *Organizaţiile obşteşti în sistemul organizarii politice din Republica Socialistă România.* Bucureşti: Editura Academiei Republicii Socialiste România, 1973.

Almond, Gabriel, ed. *Comparative Politics Today: A World View.* Boston: Little, Brown and Co., 1974.

Anderson, C.W.; von der Mehden, F.R.; and Young, C. *Issues of Political Development.* Englewood Cliffs, N.J.: Prentice-Hall, 1974.

Anderson, L.F.; Watts, W.W., Jr.,; and Wilcox, A.R. *Legislative Roll-Call Analysis.* Evanston, Ill.: Northwestern University Press, 1966.

Applebaum, Richard P. *Theories of Social Change.* Chicago, Ill.: Markham, 1970.

Apter, David E. *Politics of Modernization.* Chicago: University of Chicago Press, 1965.

Avtorkhanov, Abdurakham. *The Communist Party Apparatus.* Cleveland: Meridian, 1968.

Beck, Carl, et al. *Comparative Communist Political Leadership.* New York: David McKay, 1973.

Beck, Carl, and Mesa-Lago, Carmelo, eds. *Comparative Socialist Systems.* Pittsburgh: UCIS, 1975.

Bill, James A., and Hardgrave, Robert L. *Comparative Politics: The Quest for Theory.* Columbus, Ohio: Charles E. Merrill, 1973.

Binder, Leonard; Coleman, James S.; et al. *Crises and Sequences in Political Development.* Princeton: Princeton University Press, 1971.

Black, Cyril E. *The Dynamics of Modernization.* New York: Harper and Row, 1966.

Bibliography 177

Blalock, Hubert M. *Social Statistics.* New York: McGraw-Hill, 1960.

Bobocea, Gheorghe, și Vlad, Stan. *Preocupările și sarcinile actuale ale consiliilor populare.* București: Editura Politica, 1969.

Bornstein, M., ed. *Plan and Market: Economic Reform in Eastern Europe.* New Haven: Yale University Press, 1973.

Boroș, Valentina. *Județele României Socialiste.* București: Editura Politica, 1972.

Bromke, Adam, and Rakowska-Harmstone, Teresa, eds. *The Communist States in Disarray.* Minneapolis: University of Minnesota Press, 1972.

Brunner, Ronald D., and Brewer, Garry D. *Organized Complexity.* New York: Free Press, 1971.

Brzezinski, Zbigniew. *The Permanent Purge: Politics in Soviet Political Succession in the USSR.* New York: Columbia University Press, 1965.

Brzezinski, Zbigniew. *The Soviet Bloc.* Cambridge: Harvard University Press, 1969.

Buletin statistic trimestrial. București: Directia Centrala de Statistica, 1957-1965.

Ceaușescu, Nicolae. *Roumania on the Way of Building up the Multilaterally Developed Socialist Society.* Vols. 1-8. Bucharest: Meridiane, 1969-1973.

Coleman, James. *Crises and Sequences in Political Development.* Princeton: Princeton University Press, 1971.

Cornell, Richard, ed. *The Soviet Political System: A Book of Readings.* Englewood Cliffs, N.J.: Prentice-Hall, 1970.

Dahrendorf, Ralf. *Class and Class Conflict in Industrial Society.* Stanford: Stanford University Press, 1959.

Demeter, J.; Eisenburger, E.E.; and Lipatti, V. *Romania and the National Question.* Bucharest: Meridiane, 1972.

Draganu, Tudor. *Formele de activitate ale Organelor Statului Socialist Român.* București: Editura Politica, 1965.

Farrell, R. Barry, ed. *Political Leadership in Eastern Europe and the Soviet Union.* Chicago: Aldine, 1970.

Finkle, J.L., and Gable, R.W., eds. *Political Development and Social Change.* New York: John Wiley and Sons, 1971.

Fischer-Galati, Stephen. *The New Romania.* Cambridge, Mass.: M.I.T. Press, 1970.

Fischer-Galati, Stephen. *The Socialist Republic of Romania.* Baltimore: Johns Hopkins University Press, 1970.

178   BIBLIOGRAPHY

Gorden, Morton. *Comparative Political Systems: Managing Conflict.*
New York: The Macmillan Co., 1972.

Groth, Alexander J. *Comparative Politics: A Distributive Approach.*
New York: The Macmillan Co., 1971.

Hammer, Darrell P. *U.S.S.R.: The Politics of Oligarchy.* Hinsdale, Illin-
ois: The Dryden Press, 1974.

Holt, Dimitru. *Formele de Legatura a sfaturilor populare şi a comitetelor
lor executive cu masele.* Bucureşti: Editura Ştînţifica, 1962.

Holt, Dimitru. *Administraţie de Stat în Republica Socialista România.*
Bucharest: Editura Politica, 1968.

Holt, Robert, and Turner, John. *The Political Basis of Economic Development.* Princeton: Van Nostrand, 1966.

Holt, Robert. *The Methodology of Comparative Research.* New York:
The Free Press, 1970.

Huntington, Samuel P. *Political Order in Changing Societies.* New Haven,
Conn.: Yale University Press, 1968.

Ionescu, Ghiţa. *Communism in Rumania, 1944-1962.* London: 1964.

Ionescu, Ghiţa. *The Politics of the European Communist States.* New
York: Praeger, 1967.

Johnson, Chalmers, ed. *Change in Communist Systems.* Stanford: Stanford University Press, 1970.

Kautsky, John H. *The Political Consequences of Modernization.* New
York: John Wiley and Sons, 1972.

Kautsky, John H. *Communism and Political Development.* New York:
John Wiley and Sons, 1968.

King, R.R., and Dean, R.W., eds. *Eastern European Perspectives of European Security and Cooperation.* New York: Praeger, 1974.

Kornberg, Allan, and Musolf, Lloyd D., eds. *Legislatures in Developmental
Perspectives.* Durham, N.C.: Duke University Press, 1970.

Lane, David. *Politics and Society in the USSR.* New York: Random
House, 1971.

LaPalombara, Joseph, ed. *Bureaucracy and Political Development.* Prince-
ton:Princeton University Press, 1963.

Lendvai, Paul. *Eagles in Cobwebs.* Garden City, N.Y.: Doubleday, 1969.

Lenin, V.I. *On Party Construction.* Moscow, 1956.

Lepadatescu, Mircea. *Sistemul Organelor Statului în Republica Socialista
România.* Bucureşti: Editura Ştiinţifica, 1966.

Bibliography

179

Levy, Marion. *Modernization and the Structure of Societies.* Princeton: Princeton University Press, 1966.

Leys, Colin, ed. *Politics and Change in Developing Countries.* Cambridge: Cambridge University Press, 1969.

Ludz, Peter C. *The Changing Party Elite in East Germany.* Cambridge, Mass.: M.I.T. Press, 1973.

Mazilu, Dumitru, I. *Funcţiile statului socialist.* Bucureşti: Editura Academiei Republicii Socialiste Româna, 1972.

Meyer, Alfred E. *The Soviet Political System.* New York: Random House, 1965.

Milbrath, L.W. *Political Participation.* Chicago: Rand-McNally, 1965.

Moore, W.E. *Social Change.* Englewood Cliffs, N.J.: Prentice-Hall, 1963.

Negoîta, Alexandru. *Organele Obşteşti cu Atribuţii Jurisdicţionale în R.S.R.* Cluj: Grafica Nova II, 1967.

Negoîta, Alexandru. *Ştiinţa Administraţiei.* Bucureşti: Universitatea Bucureşti, 1972.

Osborne, Robert J. *The Evolution of Soviet Politics.* Homewood, Ill.: Dorsey Press, 1974.

Pirages, Dennis. *Modernization and Political Tension-Management: A Socialist Society in Perspective.* New York: Praeger, 1972.

Pye, Lucian. *Aspects of Political Development.* Boston: Little, Brown and Co., 1966.

Pye, Lucian, and Verba, Sidney, eds. *Political Culture and Political Development.* Princeton: Princeton University Press, 1966.

Riggs, Fred W. *Administration in Developing Countries: The Theory of Prismatic Society.* Boston: Houghton Mifflin, 1964.

Rokkan, Stein, ed. *Comparative Research Across Cultures and Nations.* The Hague: Mouton, 1968.

Schapiro, Leonard. *The Communist Party of the Soviet Union.* New York: Vintage, 1971.

Schmitt, David E. *Dynamics of the Third World.* Cambridge: Wintrop, 1974.

Siegel, Sidney. *Nonparametric Statistics.* New York: McGraw-Hill, 1956.

Skilling, H. Gordon. *The Governments of Communist East Europe.* New York: Thomas Crowell, 1966.

Stalin, J.V. *Problems of Leninism.* Moscow, 1947.

Stanel, S., and Cucui, N. *Deputatul Sfatului Popular-activist obştesc.* Bucureşti: Editura Politică, 1962.

180   BIBLIOGRAPHY

Trasnea, Ovidiu, and Voiculescu, Marin, eds. *Studii de Ştiinţa Politica.*
    Bucureşti: Editura Politica, 1973. Vol. IX de Teorie şi Metoda în
    Ştiinţele Sociale.
Triska, Jan F., ed. *Communist Party-States.* Indianapolis: Bobbs-Merrill,
    1969.
Vîntu, Ion; Anghene, Mircea; and Straoanu, Micrea. *Organele Adminis-*
    traţiei de Stat în Republica Socialistă România. Bucureşti: Editura
    Academiei Republicii Socialiste România, 1971.
Vîntu, Ion; Lepadatescu, M.; Merlescu, I.; and Anghene, M. *Sfaturile*
    Populare: Organe Locale ale Puterii de Stat în RPR. Bucureşti:
    Editura Academiei RPR, 1964.
Welch, Claude E., ed. *Political Modernization.* Belmont, California: Wads-
    worth, 1967.

ARTICLES, SPEECHES

Anghene, Mircea. "Elemente Privind Conducerea, Ştiinţifica în Adminis-
    traţia de State." *Studii şi Cercetări Juridice,* Nr. 1 (1971).
Anghene, Mircea. "Organele Locale de Specialitate ale Administraţiei de
    State." *Revista Româna de Drept,* Nr. 6 (1970).
Apostol, P. "Domeniul Ştiinţei Conducerii Societăţii Socialiste." *Ştiinţa*
    Conducerii Societaţii. Bucureşti: Editura Politica, 1971.
Bascom, William. "Urbanizing Among the Yoruba." *The American Journal*
    of Sociology. Vol. 60, 1955.
Blajovic, Petre. "Cerinţe noi în Organizarea Teritoriala şi Sistematizarea
    Rurala,"*Probleme Economice,* Nr. 11 (1967).
Bobocea, Gheorghe. "Organizarea administrative-teritoriala—factor organi-
    zator al vieţii social-economice," *Lupta de Clasa,* Nr. 11 (1967).
Boldur, Gheorghe. "Informaţia şi decizia în procesul conducerii social-
    economice." *Ştiinţa Conducerii Societaţii.* Bucureşti: Editura Poli-
    tica, 1971.
Brown, Alan A., and Marer, Paul. "Foreign Trade in the East European
    Reforms," in *Plan and Market,* M. Bornstein, ed. New Haven: Yale
    University Press, 1973.
Brown, J.F. "Soviet Policy in Eastern Europe and the Impact of Detente,"
    in *Eastern European Perspectives on European Security and Cooper-*
    ation, R.R. King and R.W. Dean, eds. New York: Praeger, 1974.

Bibliography 181

Ceaușescu, N. *Cuvîntare la prima Conferința pe țară a secretarilor comitetelor de partid și a președinților consiliilor populare comunale, December 23, 1971.* București: Editura Politică, 1971.

Ceaușescu, N. "Opening Remarks to the Collo!uium on Problems of the Science of Social Management, 6 March 1972." *Viitorul Social* (Septembrie, 1972).

Ceaușescu, N. *Raport la cel de-al X-lea Congres al Partidului Comunist Român, 6 August. 1969.* București: Editura Politică, 1969.

Ceaușescu, N. *Raport la Conferința Naționala a Partidului Comunist Român, December, 1967.* București: Editura Politică, 1967.

Ceaușescu, N. *Raport la Conferința Naționala a Partidului Comunist Român 19-21 iulie 1972.* București: Editura Politică, 1972.

Ceaușescu, N. *Raportul cu privire la măsurile de perfecționare a conducerii și planificării economiei naționale și la imbunătătirea organizării administrativ-teritoriale a României, 6 Decembrie, 1967.* București: Meridiane, 1967.

Ceaușescu, N. "Speech at the Working Meeting of the Party Active from the Sphere of Ideology and Political and Cultural-Educational Activity," in Supplement to *Romania Today* (9 July 1971).

Ceterchi, Ioan. "Organizarea de Stat și Formarea de Cadre in R.S.R." *Analele Universitații București, Seria Știinte Juridice,* Nr. 2 (1970).

Churchward, L.G. "Soviet Local Government Today." *Soviet Studies,* XVII, No. 4 (April, 1966).

Eckstein, A. "Economic Development and Political Change in Communist Systems," in *World Politics* 22 (July 1970).

Edeen, Alf. "The Administrative Intelligentsia." *Survey,* No. 65 (October 1967).

Fischer, Gabriel, "Romania," in *The Communist States in Disarray,* ed. Adam Bromke and Teresa Rakowska-Harmstone. Minneapolis: University of Minnesota, 1972.

Fleron, Frederic J. "Co-optation as a Mechanism of Adaptation to Change: The Soviet Political Leadership System." *Polity,* II (1969).

Huntington, Samuel P. "Political Development and Political Decay," *World Politics,* XVII (1965).

Huntington, Samuel P. "The Change to Change." *Comparative Politics* (April, 1971).

BIBLIOGRAPHY

LaPalombara, Joseph. "Parsimony and Empiricism in Comparative Politics: An Anti-Scholastic View," in *The Methodology of Comparative Research*, ed. R.T. Holt and J.E. Turner. New York: Free Press, 1970.

Lerner, Daniel. "Comparative Analysis of Processes of Modernization," in *Comparative Research Across Cultures and Nations*, ed. Stein Rokkan. The Hague: Mouton, 1968.

Lowenthal, Richard. "Development vs. Utopia in Communist Policy," in *Change in Communist Systems*, Chalmers Johnson, ed. Stanford: Stanford University Press, 1970.

Nie, Norman H.; Powell, G. Bingham, Jr.; and Prewitt, Kenneth. "Social Structure and Political Participation: Developmental Relationships, I and II." *The American Political Science Review*. Vol. 63, June and September, 1969.

Nucercu, E. "Legislația și cerințele vieții sociale." *Lupta de Clasa*, Nr. 3 (1968).

Patulea, V. "Schimbarea conținutului social-politic al legislației în 20 de ani de Republica Socialista." *Revista Româna de Drept*, Nr. 12 (1967).

Pirages, Dennis. "Socioeconomic Development and Political Access in the Communist Party-States," in *Communist Party-States*, Jan F. Triska, ed. Indianapolis: Bobbs-Merrill, 1969.

Powell, John D. "Peasant Society and Clientelist Politics." *The American Political Science Review*, 64 (June, 1970).

Pye, Lucian W. "Identity and the Political Culture," in *Crises and Sequences in Political Development*, Leonard Binder, et al. Princeton: Princeton Universtiy Press, 1971.

Rausser, Vasile. "Romania's Economic Relations with the Developing Countries." *Revue Roumaine des Sciences Sociales: Serie de Sciences Economiques* (Tome 16, No. 2, 1972).

Rush, Keith. "The Reforms: A Balance Sheet." *Problems of Communism* (July-August, 1967).

Scott, James C. "Corruption, Machine Politics, and Political Change." *American Political Science Review*, 62 (December, 1969).

Tamaș, S. "Prospectarea în Procesul Conducerii." *Știința Conducerii Societații*. București: Editura Politică, 1971.

Tarrow, S. "The Urban-Rural Cleavage in Political Involvement." *The American Political Science Review*, 65 (June, 1971).

Bibliography 183

Triska, Jan F. and Johnson, Paul M. "Political Development and Political Change," in Carmelo Mesa-Lago and Carl Beck, eds., *Comparative Socialist Systems.* Pittsburgh: UCIS (1975).

Vîntu, Ion. "Centralisme et autonomie." *Res Publica.* Vol. XIII, No. 5 (1971).

Vîntu, Ion. "Romania," in *Central Services to Local Authorities in Selected Eastern European Countries and the USSR.* New York: The United Nations, 1970.

Vîntu, Ion. "Reorganization of Administrative Structure in Romania." *Studies in Comparative Local Government.* (November, 1968).

Weingrod, Alex. "Patrons, Patronage and Political Parties." *Comparative Studies in Society and History.* Vol. 10 (July, 1969).

Welsh, William A. "Introduction," in *Comparative Communist Political Leadership,* Carl Beck, et al. New York: David McKay, 1973.

Welsh, William A. "Toward a Multiple-Strategy Approach to Research on Comparative Communist Political Elites: Empirical and Qualitative Problems," in *Communist Studies and the Social Sciences: Essays on Methodology and Empirical Theory,* Frederic J. Fleron, Jr., ed. Chicago: Rand McNally, 1969.

DOCUMENTS AND REFERENCES

Anuarul Statistic al Republicii Socialiste România. Bucureşti: Direcţia Centrala de Statistică, 1966, 1969, 1971, 1972.

Buletinul Oficial al Republicii Socialiste România. Buletinul Oficial Iaşiului. Iaşi: Redacţia şi Administraţia Consiliul Popular al Judeţului Iaşi, Comitetul Executive.

Buletinul Oficial. Timişoara: Redacţia şi Administraţia al Consiliul Popular al Judeţului Timiş.

Conferinţa pe Ţara a Secretarilor Comitetelor de Partid şi a Preşedinţilor Consiliilor Populare Comunale, 1971. *Resoluţia Conferinţa pe ţara a secretarilor comitetelor de partid şi a preşedinţilor consiliilor populare comunale.* Bucureşti: Editura Politică, 1972.

Die Volksrate–Die Politische Grundlage der Rumänischen Volksrepublik. Bukarest: F. Editura, 1953.

Frontul Unitaţii Socialiste. *Documente Constitutive.* Bucureşti: Editura Politică, 1969.

184   BIBLIOGRAPHY

*Instrucţiuni pentru darile de seama ce se completeaza de care comitetele
    executive ale consiliilor populare cominale în anul 1970.* Bucureşti:
    Direcţia Centrala de Statista, 1970.
Partidul Comunist Român. "Declaraţie cu privire la poziţia Partidului
    Muncitoresc Român în Problemele cişcarii Comuniste şi Muncitoreşti
    internaţionale adoptata de Plenara largita a C.C. al P.M.R. din Aprilie,
    1964." Bucureşti: Editura Politică, 1964.
Partidul Comunist Român. (Plenara). "Princiipiile de baza adoptate de
    plenara C.C. al P.C.R. din 5-6 Octombrie 1967 cu privire la îmbuna-
    taţirea organizarii administrativ teritoriale a României şi sistem-
    atizarea localitaţilor rurale," in *Proiect.* Bucureşti: Editura Politică,
    1967.
Partidul Comunist Român. "Directivele Conferinţei Naţionale e Partidu-
    lui Comunist Român cu Privire la Sistematizarea Teritoriului, a
    Oraşelor şi Satelor, la Dezvoltarea lor economico-socială," in *Confer-
    inţa Naţională a Partidului Comunist Român.* Bucureşti: Editura
    Politică, 1972.
Partidul Comunist Român. *Documente ale Partidului Comunist Roman:
    Perfecţionarea organizarii şi conducerii vieţii sociale, Rolul Statului
    Socialist.* Bucureşti: Editura Politică, 1972.
Partidul Comunist Român. "Rezoluţia Conferinţei Naţionale a Partidului
    Comunist Român cu privire la perfecţionarea organizarii şi Con-
    ducerii vieţii Sociale şi la Dezvoltarea Democraţiei Socialiste," in
    Conferinţa Nationala a Partidului Comunist Român. Bucureşti:
    Editura Politică, 1972.
Partidul Comunist Român. *Principii şi Norme ale Organizarii şi Activitaţii
    Partidului Comunist Român.* Bucureşti: Editura Politică, 1972.
Partidul Comunist Român. "Rezoluţia Congresului al X-lea al Partidului
    Comunist Român." Bucureşti: Editura Politică, 1969.
Partidul Comunist Român. *Statutul Partidului Comunist Român.* Bucu-
    reşti: Editura Politică, 1969.
România, Legi şi Decrete. *Constitution of the Socialist Republic of
    Romania.* Bucureşti: Meridiane, 1969.
România, Legi şi Decrete. *Decret pentru organizarea şi funcţionarea
    sfaturilor populare.* Bucureşti: Editura de Stat, 1950.
România, Legi şi Decrete. *Organizing and Functioning Law of the People's
    Councils* (voted by the Grand National Assembly on December 26,

Bibliography 185

1968), in *Bulletin of the Socialist Republic of Romania.* Part I, No. 168 (December 26, 1968).

România, Legi și Decrete. *Regulamentul de funcționare a sfatului popular al orașului de subordonare republicană.* București: Editura de Stat, 1950.

România, Legi și Decrete. *Regumental de funcționare a Sfaturilor Populare Raionale.* București: Editura de Stat, 1950.

România, Legi și Decrete. *Standing Orders of the Grand National Assembly.* Bucharest: Meridiane, 1969.

România, Legi și Decrete. *The Law No. 28/1966 Regulating the Election of Deputies to the Grand National Assembly and the People's Councils.* Bucharest: Meridiane, 1969.

United Nations. *Central Services to Local Authorities in Selected Eastern European Countries and the Union of Soviet Socialist Republics.* New York: United Nations, 1970.

United States Congress, 91st, 2nd Session, Joint Economic Committee. *Economic Developments in Countries of Eastern Europe.* Washington, D.C.: GPO, 1970.

World Bank Atlas. Washington, D.C.: International Bank for Reconstruction and Development, 1972.

ROMANIAN PERIODICALS CONSULTED

Din Experiența Sfaturilor Populare (Anul I-XIII, 1956-1968).

Drapelul Roșu. Organ al comitetlului Județean Timiș al P.C.R. și al Consiliului Popular Județean.

Drum Nou. Organ al Comitetului Județean Brașov al P.C.R. și al Consiliului Popular Județean.

Faclia. Organ al Comitetului Județean Cluj al P.C.R. și al Consiliului Popular Județean.

Flacara Iașului. Organ al Comitetului Județean Iași al P.C.R. și al Consiliului Popular Județean.

Lupta de Clasa.

Problemeale Administrației Locale (Anul XIII-XIV, 1968-1969).

Probleme ale Consiliilor Populare, ale Economiei și Administrației Locale de Stat (Anul XIV-XVIII, 1969-1973)î earlier (1956-June, 1968) known as Din *Experiența Sfaturilor Populare* and (July, 1968-

December, 1969) *Probleme ale Administraţiei Locale.*
Probleme Economice.
Revista Româna de Drept. Organ al asociaţiei Juriştilor din Republica
    Socialista România.
Revue Roumaine des Sciences Sociales: Serie de Sciences Economiques.
Romania: Documents—Events. Vols. IV-V.
Scînteia. Organ al Comitetului Central al Partidului Comunist Român
    (Anul XLII-1973).
Scînteia Tineretului.
Studii şi Cercetari Juridice (Anul 13-18).
Tinarul Leninist.
Viitorul Social.

EAST EUROPEAN MONOGRAPHS

The *East European Monographs* comprise scholarly books on the history and civilization of Eastern Europe. They are published by the *East European Quarterly* in the belief that these studies contribute substantially to the knowledge of the area and serve to stimulate scholarship and research.

Political Ideas and the Enlightenment in the Romanian Principalities, 17501831. By Vlad Georgescu. 1971.

America, Italy and the Birth of Yugoslavia, 1917-1919. By Dragan R. Zivjinovic. 1972.

Jewish Nobles and Geniuses in Modern Hungary. By William O. McCagg,Jr. 1972.

Mixail Soloxov in Yugoslavia: Reception and Literary Impact. By Robert F. Price. 1973.

The Historical and National Thought of Nicolae Iorga. By William O. Oldson. 1973.

Guide to Polish Libraries and Archives. By Richard C. Lewanski. 1974.

Vienna Broadcasts to Slovakia, 1938-1939: A Case Study in Subversion. By Henry Delfiner. 1974.

The 1917 Revolution in Latvia. By Andrew Ezergailis. 1974.

The Ukraine in the United Nations Organization: A Study in Soviet Foreign Policy. 1944-1950. By Konstantin Sawczuk. 1975.

The Bosnian Church: A New Interpretation. By John V. A. Fine, Jr., 1975.

Intellectual and Social Developments in the Habsburg Empire from Maria Theresa to World War I. Edited by Stanley B. Winters and Joseph Held. 1975.

Ljudevit Gaj and the Illyrian Movement. By Elinor Murray Despalatovic. 1975.

Tolerance and Movements of Religious Dissent in Eastern Europe. Edited by Bela K. Kiraly. 1975.

The Parish Republic: Hlinka's Slovak People's Party, 19391945. By Yeshayahu Jelinek. 1976.

The Russian Annexation of Bessarabia, 1774-1828. By George F. Jewsbury. 1976.

Modern Hungarian Historiography. By Steven Bela Vardy. 1976.

Values and Community in Multi-National Yugoslavia. By Gary K. Bertsch. 1976.

The Greek Socialist Movement and the First World War: the Road to unity. By George B. Leon. 1976.

The Radical Left in the Hungarian Revolution of 1848. By Laszlo Deme. 1976.

Hungary between Wilson and Lenin: The Hungarian Revolution of 1918-1919 and the Big Three. By Peter Pastor. 1976.

The Crises of France's East-Central European Diplomacy, 1933-1938. By Anthony J. Komjathy. 1976.

Polish Politics and National aReform, 1775-1788. By Daniel Stone. 1976.

The Habsburg Empire in World War I. Robert A. Kann, Bela K. Kiraly, and Paula S. Fichtner, eds. 1977.

The Slovenes and Yugoslavism, 1890-1914. By Carole Rogel. 1977.

German-Hungarian Relations and the Swabian Problem. By Thomas Spira. 1977.

The Metamorphosis of a Social Class in Hungary During the Reign of Young Franz Joseph. By Peter I. Hidas. 1977.

Tax Reform in Eighteenth Century Lombardy. By Daniel M. Klang. 1977.

*Tradition versus Revolution: Russia and the Balkans in 1917.*By Robert H. Johnston. 1977.

Winter into Spring: The Czechoslovak Press and the Reform Movement 19631968. By Frank L. Kaplan. 1977.

The Catholic Church and the Soviet Government, 1939-1949. By Dennis J. Dunn. 1977.

*The Hungarian Labor Service System, 1939-1945.*By Randolph L Braham. 1977.

Consciousness and History: Nationalist Critics of Greek Society 1897-1914. By Gerasimos Augustinos. 1977.

Emigration in Polish Social and Political Thought, 1870-1914. By Benjamin P. Murdzek. 1977.

Serbian Poetry and Milutin Bojic. By Mihailo Dordevic. 1977.

The Baranya Dispute: Diplomacy in the Vortex of Ideologies, 1918-1921. By Leslie C. Tihany. 1978.

The United States in Prague, 1945-1948. By Walter Ullmann. 1978.

Rush to the Alps: The Evolution of Vacationing in Switzerland. By Paul P. Bernard. 1978.

Transportation in Eastern Europe: Empirical Findings. By Bogdan Mieczkowski. 1978.

The Polish Underground State: A Guide to the Underground, 1939-1945. By Stefan Korbónski. 1978.

The Hungarian Revolution of 1956 in Retrospect. Edited by Bela K. Kiraly and Paul Jonas. 1978.

Boleslaw Limanowski (1835-1935): A Study in Socialism and Nationalism. By Kazimiera Janina Cottam. 1978.

The Lingering Shadow of Nazism: The Austrian Independent Party Movement Since 1945. By Max E. Riedlsperger. 1978.

The Catholic Church, Dissent and Nationality in Soviet Lithuania. By V. Stanley Vardys. 1978.

The Development of Parliamentary Government in Serbia. By Alex N. Dragnich. 1978.

Divide and Conquer: German Efforts to Conclude a Separate Peace, 1914-1918. By L. L. Farrar, Jr. 1978.

The Prague Slav Congress of 1848. By Lawrence D. Orton. 1978.

The Nobility and the Making of the Hussite Revolution. By John M. Klassen. 1978.

The Cultural Limits of Revolutionary politics: Change and Continuity in Socialist Czechoslovakia. By David W. Paul. 1979.

On the Border of War and Peace: Polish Intelligence and Diplomacy in 19371939 and the Origins of the Ultra Secret. By Richard A. Woytak. 1979.

Bear and Foxes: The International Relations of the East European States 19651969. By Ronald Haly Linden. 1979.

Cxechoslovakia: The Heritage of Ages Past. Edited by Ivan Volgyes and Hans Brisch. 1979.

Prima Minister Gyula Andrassy's Influence on Habsburg Foreign Policy. By Janos Decsy. 1979.

Citizens for the Fatherland: Education, Educators, and Pedagogical ideals in Eighteenth Century Russia. By J. L. Black. 1979.

A History of the "Proletariat": The Emergence of Marxism in the Kingdom of Poland, 1870-1887. By Norman M. Naimark. 1979.

The Slovak Autonomy Movement, 1935-1939: A Study in Unrelenting Nationalism. By Dorothea H. El Mallakh. 1979.

Diplomat in Exile: Francis Pulszky's Political Activities in England, 1849-1860. By Thomas Kabdebo. 1979.

The German Struggle Against the Yugoslav Guerrillas in World War II: German Counter-Insurgency in Yugoslavia, 1941-1943. By Paul N. Hehn. 1979.

The Emergence of the Romanian National State. By Gerald J. Bobango. 1979.

Stewards of the Land: The American Farm School and Modern Greece. By Brenda L. Marder. 1979.

Roman Dmowski: Party, Tactics, ideology, 1895-1907. By Alvin M. Fountain, II. 1980.

International and Domestic Politics in Greece During the Crimean War. By Jon V. Kofas. 1980.

Fires on the Mountain: The Macedonian Revolutionary Movement and the Kidnapping of Ellen Stone. By Laura Beth Sherman. 1980.

The Modernization of Agriculture: Rural Transformation in Hungary, 18481975. Edited by Joseph held. 1980.

Britain and the War for Yugoslavia, 1940-1943. By Mark C. Wheeler. 1980.

The Turn to the Right: The Odeological Origins and Development of Ukrainian Nationalism, 1919-1929. By Alexander J. Motyl. 1980.

The Maple Leaf and the White Eagle: Canadian-Polish Relations, 1918-1978. By Aloysius Balawyder. 1980.

Antecedents of Revolution: Alexander I and the Polish Congress Kingdom, 1815-1825. By Frank W. Thackeray. 1980.

Blood Libel at Tiszaeszlar. By Andrew Handler. 1980.

Democratic Centralism in Romania: A Study of Local Communist Politics. By Daniel N. Nelson. 1980.

The Challenge of Communist Education: A Look at the German Democratic Republic. By Margrete Siebert Klein, 1980.

The Fortifications and Defense of Constantinople. By Byron C.P. Tsangadas. 1980.

Balkan Cultural Studies. By Stavro Skendi. 1980.

Studies in Ethnicity: The East European Experience in America. Edited by Charles A. Ward, Philip Shahshko, and Donald E. Pienkos. 1980.

The Logic of "Normalization:" The soviet Intervention in Czechoslovakia and the Czechoslovak Response. By Fred Eidlin. 1980.